[signature]
Boston
January 12th 1995

PROTESTANTISM
AND
PRIMOGENITURE
IN
EARLY MODERN
GERMANY

PAULA SUTTER FICHTNER

PROTESTANTISM AND PRIMOGENITURE IN EARLY MODERN GERMANY

YALE UNIVERSITY PRESS
NEW HAVEN AND LONDON

Set in Garamond No. 3 type by The Composing Room of Michigan, Inc. Printed in the United States of America by Vail-Ballou Press, Binghamton, New York.

Library of Congress Cataloging-in-Publication Data
Fichtner, Paula S.
Protestantism and primogeniture in early modern Germany / Paula Sutter Fichtner.
p.   cm.
Bibliography: p.
Includes index.
ISBN 0-300-04425-9 (alk. paper) : $22.50
1. Primogeniture—Germany—History.
2. Inheritance and succession—Germany—History.
3. Germany—Kings and rulers. 4. Reformation—Germany.   I. Title.
KK301.B57F53   1989
346.4305'2—dc19
[344.30652]   89-5487
                                                    CIP

The paper in this book meets the guidelines for permanence and durability of the Committee on Production Guidelines for Book Longevity of the Council on Library Resources.

10   9   8   7   6   5   4   3   2   1

Milton Joseph Sutter, Jr.
In memoriam

CONTENTS

ACKNOWLEDGMENTS

This study grew from a paper delivered at the Metropolitan Museum of Art in New York in January 1979. The occasion was a symposium connected with an exhibition from the Dresden *Kunstkammer* traveling through the United States. The talk was given at the invitation of Dr. Ann Sutherland Harris, then chairperson for academic affairs at the museum; I would once again like to thank her for prompting me to begin work on this book.

Subsequent papers, more narrowly focused on the issues of partible inheritance, religious belief, and state building in Germany, were given before the Seminar in the History of Legal and Political Thought and Institutions of Columbia University and at the annual conference of the Sixteenth Century Studies Association in 1984. As a panel commentator at the latter, the late James Allen Vann offered a searching and useful critique of the presentation.

The staffs of the Tyrolean *Landesarchiv* in Innsbruck, the Bavarian State Archives, the Hessian State Archives in Marburg, and the Austrian *Haus-, Hof-, und Staatsarchiv* in Vienna were also most helpful. I am especially indebted to Dr. Gerhard Menk in Marburg for the cordial cooperation I found there and to S. K. H. Duke Albrecht of Bavaria and Dr. Andreas von Majewski for a similar reception accorded me in Munich at the *Geheimes Hausarchiv*. Dr. Christiane Thomas was, as always, an invaluable resource for me in Vienna.

Many colleagues have been enlisted as bibliographic informants, as sounding boards, and as critics. All were helpful, but particular mention must go to Minna Cardoza, James C. Davis, William F.

Jannen, Jr., Bodo Nischan, and John and Danila Spielman. Edward Fichtner gave valuable linguistic and technical support. Ruth Kleinman ploughed staunchly through all the major drafts of the manuscript, chiding where chiding was due, and encouraging where such was very much needed. To all the above I owe my thanks and my apologies for whatever shortcomings still lurk in the text despite so much expert advice.

INTRODUCTION

Reformation historians have long wrestled with the task of distinguishing the traditional from the innovative in Martin Luther's theology and ecclesiology. The new confession clearly wrought fundamental changes in church organization and sacerdotal function. Yet the Lutheran reform owed so much to medieval piety that one can call it radical only by ignoring some of its most distinctive features.

But should the question turn to the influence Lutheranism exercised on German political thought and practice, scholars who are secularly inclined have reached far greater consensus. Indeed, it has become a venerable truism among German historians and students of political theory in general that German Protestantism, especially Lutheranism, enabled many territorial princes to fulfill absolutist ambitions of long standing. Kings and princes, as Luther himself remarked in 1530, were no less the servants of God than anyone else; in performing their duties, they were doing the work of the Lord. The subject had few alternatives but to obey. The break with Rome put the supervision of educational and charitable institutions and the territorial church itself into the hands of the German Protestant ruler. Out of this context arose the confessionally organized, patriarchal German principality of the early modern era, the so-called *Polizeistaat*. The *Landesherren* of these polities, such as Landgrave William IV of Hesse-Kassel (1532–1592) or Duke Ernest the Pious of Saxony-Gotha (1601–1675), guided the public and private behavior of their peoples down to the last detail. Their eagerness to spread the new faith and constant vigilance against Catholic aggression gave the Protestants military experience that would also prove useful in future efforts to consolidate their political position. The next phase of this development, or so the analysis goes, would be the absolute territorial ruler of the eighteenth century— Frederick William I (1688–1740) and Frederick the Great (1712–1786) of Prussia are the archexamples. Such men were largely free of religious scruples in politics and diplomacy but, because of the religious associations that their role evoked, were nevertheless able to command automatic obedience from subject and local institutions alike.[1] In its crudest form, this picture of Protestantism, especially Lutheranism, and its association with German territorial absolutism has often been used to explain an alleged national bent for authoritarian government—William L. Shirer's widely read *The Rise and Fall of the Third Reich* comes quickly to mind. But far more discerning students of German and administrative history have believed, and still do, that Protestantism and German absolutism were mutually supportive.[2]

It is true that more recent scholarship has begun to approach this question somewhat more subtly. Distinctions are now drawn, for example, between Luther, the thinker and theologian, and the institutional structure of Lutheranism, which allowed the German princes to tighten their administrative control of their territories. Luther, according to this version, was not altogether pleased with the seeming natural affinity between a prince's *ius reformandi* and state building. Rather he resigned himself to the development, believing that little could be done about it. Nor can it be so confidently claimed that Lutheran princes alone put their faith to such purposes. Catholicism played a similar role in areas such as Bavaria and the Habsburg Tyrol. Calvinism, too, which has traditionally enjoyed a somewhat better press in the West because of perceived connections with representative government, was not immune to this tendency. Thus what is called the "confessionalization" of not only the German lands but a great deal of Europe was crucial to the development of the centralized modern state.[3]

It is clear that all of the major confessions contributed heavily to the growth of the seventeenth-century *Polizeistaat*. Nor can one deny that many German religious and political polemicists have fostered the idea that Reformation Protestantism and a strong, unified, and "Christian" Germany are inextricably linked. As the notorious nineteenth-century anti-Semitic pastor Adolf Stoecker put it following the creation of the Second Empire in 1871, "The Holy German Protestant Empire is now achieved, . . . and in it we can trace the hand of God from 1517 to 1871." More explicitly sinister was the comment of the German Evangelical Union six days after Hitler's Enabling Act of 1933: "In the midst of the national movement of these days, one thing must not be forgotten: what is built now can only be built in harmony with the most momentous German national movement of all time, the German Reformation, and in the spirit of the greatest German of all time, Martin Luther."[4]

Protestantism, including Lutheranism, has been vigorously defended against charges of encouraging political passivity among its faithful. But these arguments are usually made by citing instances of Protestant resistance to state authority—by Puritans, Pietists, or late sixteenth-century Lutheran burghers in Lippe.[5] Such discussions lead inexorably to the conclusion that Protestantism could undermine princely absolutism only when believers put themselves at odds with their ruler, supposedly as a matter of conscience. That a Protestant prince of the Reformation could be politically inconvenienced by his faith because he believed it, is rarely considered. A whole area of the complex relationship between Christianity and European society, a topic contemporary Reformation scholars are exploring ever more searchingly, thus remains unformulated, let alone investigated.

Yet, before serious historians accept Protestantism and the consolidation of princely power in Germany as two sides of the same coin or conclude that Protestant and Catholic confessional imperatives were equally useful in this process, they should look closely at a map of the early modern empire and ponder what they see. The Protestant lands will appear far more fragmented than the Catholic ones, especially in the first half of the seventeenth century, and for good reason. It was precisely the German Protestant princes who between 1525 and 1650 followed a traditional policy that in the opinion of both historians and contemporary men of affairs seriously undercut efforts to enhance their power and influence. This was the custom of partible inheritance—the division of a dynasty's private, and sometimes public, lands and titles among its legitimate male heirs. The ancient practice not only survived among many of these rulers but apparently flourished throughout the sixteenth and a good part of the seventeenth centuries. By contrast, the holdings of the leading Catholic dynasties, the Habsburgs and the Wittelsbachs, where primogeniture was firmly entrenched in the ruling house by 1650, were far less fragmented. It is therefore no accident that the burden of the detail recently used by Gerald Strauss to describe the workings of the late Reformation *Polizeistaat* comes from the Bavaria of Elector Maximilian I.[6]

Few aspects of political life in Germany before the eighteenth century seem as remote from current views of the state as partible inheritance. We accept a relatively high concentration of resources in the hands of our governments as necessary to advance the welfare of a polity, however that may be defined. With this willful redistribution of lands, both private and public, and often the dignities associated with them, as well as movables such as wine, wood, and weaponry, the German princes of the sixteenth and seventeenth centuries confound our views of rational administrative behavior. They ran afoul of other political programs as well, especially modern nationalism. In the words of a vigorous partisan of German unity in the nineteenth century:

> Attention was no longer paid to natural ties, only what was seen to be the private advantage of the princely family was decisive. The right to rule over land and people was treated merely as a matter of private law, and divisions were made solely with an eye to the comforts of those doing the dividing, not in the least to the common good. Since each brother wanted for his portion good terrain to satisfy his passion for hunting, well-stocked fish ponds for his table, productive vineyards for his cellar, even the geographical relationships of individual districts were ignored, and the whole territory was split up like a common private property.[7]

Even foreign contemporaries agreed. Evelyn Cecil, an English student of the custom, pointed to the "abyss of helplessness, confusion, and political spite [into which] the whole of the great German-speaking nation was being speedily hurled. The princes had succeeded in converting their official territories into hereditary ones, and now they were courting the suicidal epidemic of perfectly reckless subdivision."[8]

All this took place in an age when a ruler's economic, military, even political survival often hung on his ability to cobble together a centralized domain out of quasi-independent feudal units. Many modern students of German history continue to draw a sharp contrast between statesmanlike behavior on the one hand and observance of partible inheritance on the other. For such scholars, the introduction of primogeniture has become a measure of a prince's political wisdom and sense of responsibility.[9]

Nor is this link between the political immaturity and impotence of German princes and the persistence of divided inheritances among them a function of historical hindsight. Observers from the sixteenth through the eighteenth century, German and non-German, commented on the disadvantages of the practice. The philosopher Johann Gottfried von Herder, for one, urged that Prussia be apportioned among brothers as the best way of checking the growing influence of that state.[10] Yet, regardless of the damage to dynastic resources from partible inheritance many German Protestant princes routinely split their holdings among their sons and brothers until the eighteenth century. The complex nomenclatures that these divisions often created—Saxony-Gotha-Coburg, Saxony-Weimar-Eisenach, Hesse-Darmstadt-Homburg—serve even today, for the democratically minded, as archexamples of princely pretention and its absurdity.

Why should partible inheritance have lasted among rulers whose confessional stance otherwise led them to move boldly in tightening their grip on their lands and peoples? Why should the custom of primogeniture, a radical break with past practice, have become the rule far earlier in the major German houses who remained loyal to the traditional faith of Rome? If Catholic princes were simply more opportunistic than their Lutheran and Calvinist counterparts, did their religion have anything to do with their attitude? When Protestant princes as a group finally did come to see that partible inheritance and effective territorial politics did not go together, was it despite their religious beliefs? Because of them? Or did confession have no bearing on this turn of events at all? These are the issues explored in this book. It is not a study of the role of partible inheritance as such in German political history, though this will emerge as an issue. Rather, the tortuous way in which primogeniture came to be adopted in the empire will be used to advance our understanding of the impact that both Protestantism and Catholicism had on German political evolution. Accompanying this should come some greater awareness of the complex matrix of ideas and institutions that gave shape to the German territorial state. We may even gain a renewed appreciation of the role that ideas and systems of belief play in shaping the direction of events. Finally, we will certainly be reminded of something that no student of Reformation history should ever forget—that the noblest intentions can have unexpectedly perverse outcomes once they are enmeshed in the complexities of human behavior.

CHAPTER I
MEN OF
POLITICS,
MEN OF
FAITH

According to an estimate done in Vienna during the early eighteenth century, the population of Germany, including the Spanish Netherlands and Bohemia, numbered roughly twenty-eight million. Sixty-five ecclesiastical principalities, covering 14 percent of the land, governed about 12 percent of the inhabitants. Sixty imperial cities controlled only 1 percent of the land but 3-1/2 percent of the population. Imperial knights, answerable to no one other than the emperor himself, had 2 percent of the land and 1 percent of the population. Dynastic counties and lordships held sway over a further 3 percent of the empire's lands and 3 percent of those who lived there.

The overwhelming bulk of Germany's lands and people—80 percent of the former and approximately 22,500,000 of the latter—were subject to the rule of about forty-five dynastic principalities.[1] The number of these had increased steadily since the thirteenth century. It was then that the custom of dividing both the public and the private territories of a ruling house among its male members became commonplace. Among Germany's counts and lesser nobility, the practice had taken hold a century earlier.[2]

The ruling dynasties of England and France had treated their public territorial inheritances quite differently. In the former, primogeniture in the royal house appeared following the Norman invasion, as William the Conqueror and his successors set about consolidating their resources. Across the Channel, the Capetian kings of France and even their nobility had begun to observe the rule of the first born as early as the tenth century and continued to widen its application in the four hundred years to come. Even as French rulers began endowing their younger sons with appanages in the thirteenth century, a period in which large numbers of royal heirs appeared, they did not divide the crown and royal patrimony. Nor, in most cases, was there much doubt that the recipient of such a holding was subordinate to the monarch himself.[3]

The majority of the German houses proceeded otherwise. Partible inheritance of all private and even some public resources associated with princely titles remained the rule until the beginning of the eighteenth century. There were many reasons why the custom endured. Some of these were not wholly at odds with political and economic self-interest, however unlikely that may seem to modern sensibilities.

Ancient Germanic custom sanctioned the right of a prince to apportion his private holdings at will among his sons, regardless of their order of birth. There were, however, serious limitations on what any territorial ruler could do with the lands attached to whatever office he held in the empire. To qualify as an imperial prince and have a vote in the imperial diet that such a position conferred, one had to hold a fief from the German king. Such fiefs and the offices connected with them were to pass to the eldest son, a practice formally established in the law of infeudation under Frederick Barbarossa in 1158. Only if a father had a number of such fiefs could they be apportioned among sons, though the fiefs as such were to remain intact. To divide such land was to divide the title attached to it, thus, in theory, rendering the latter meaningless. Indeed, one of the reasons that counts and the lower nobility in general split their lands more frequently than princes was that they normally held no such fiefs from their sovereign.[4] Further reinforcement came to this system in Emperor Charles IV's Golden Bull of 1356, which fixed the number of imperial electors at seven. To these offices were ascribed certain lands belonging only to whoever held the electoral dignity. In the case of the secular principalities, both title and office were to be the exclusive possession of the eldest son. The private possessions of any elector, however, continued to be partible at will.[5]

In this respect, German practice did not differ materially from the French and English approach to these matters. As the fief became a functional element in the network of public authority following the Carolingian era, the right of a single person in France to both title and lands had compelling logic. The succession disputes of the Hundred Years' War confirmed the principle that the French crown was more than a proprietary possession, to be passed on regardless of gender and birth order among claimants. Under William the Conqueror and his heirs, fiefs were supposedly not given to families but to individuals whose suzerain had charged them with specific responsibilities. When such holdings became hereditary, the rule of primogeniture accompanied this development "naturally," as one writer has put it. Only through this arrangement could the holder of feudal office be sure that he had the wherewithal to carry out his public duties.[6]

But powerful pressures were at work throughout Germany in the later Middle Ages to blur this distinction between public and personal property. Anxious to wrest their independence from their king-emperor, the princes commingled their private lands with those received from their sovereign in defiant expression of their liberties. Imperial policy often helped them along. A notorious example was Emperor Frederick II's *Statutum in favorem principem* of 1232 giving territorial rulers near complete control over the internal affairs of their territories.[7] Roman law, when it finally penetrated Germany in the fourteenth century, may also have encouraged partible inheritance though the record here is more ambiguous. Jurists trained in the

Roman code argued for primogeniture among princes on the ground that the custom was compatible with their basic goal of strengthening the state. Eighteenth-century students of the law who were virtual contemporaries of the situation we are describing had a quite different opinion. For them that very same code often promoted unconditional ownership of property thereby encouraging the commingling of public and private lands. Such practices were altogether congenial to a prince anxious to dispose of all the territory under his control as he saw fit. What is of primary importance is that late medieval emperors did little to counteract this challenge to their authority, sometimes out of apathy, more often because political and economic considerations heavily compromised their bargaining position with their nominal vassals.[8]

The restrictions of the Golden Bull did not pass from memory completely. Landgrave William IV of Hesse-Kassel had them firmly in mind in 1571 as he considered strategies to follow should Elector Frederick III of the Palatine (1515–1576) die intestate. If the 1356 document and practice in the elector's own house were to be followed, Frederick's oldest son, Ludwig, would inherit both the electoral title and the lands associated with it. The reality was, as William observed, that Ludwig's brothers would want their portion, presumably from the electoral as well as private holdings, and would be supported in their request by other princes.[9] Territorial particularism had triumphed, and with it, the right of a ruler to parcel out all lands under his control as he saw fit. With few exceptions, German princely houses large and small divided and redivided their resources throughout much of the early modern era. Even after primogeniture became the rule in the early eighteenth century, several dynasties were never able to reassemble their public lands, let alone private holdings.

The princes of Anhalt, southeast of Brandenburg, executed several divisions among themselves from the twelfth century on. Briefly united in the hands of one of them, Joachim Ernest of Anhalt-Zerbst (1536–1586) in 1570, the holdings were in turn split by his sons in 1603, creating Anhalt-Zerbst, Anhalt-Dessau, Anhalt-Bernburg, and Anhalt-Cöthen. A fifth division, Anhalt-Plötzkau, was made soon after for yet another brother who had received no award in the original agreement of 1603. Plötzkau was reincorporated into the original four divisions during the course of the seventeenth century, and by the beginning of the eighteenth century primogeniture prevailed in all of the dynasty's territories. The basic divisions, however, remained.

The house of Braunschweig-Lüneburg, from which the electors of Hannover would emerge at the end of the seventeenth century, was only one of several lines into which the house of Welf had split since the Middle Ages. Wolfenbüttel introduced primogeniture in 1539; their Lüneburg relatives founded two lines—Braunschweig-Lüneburg and Braunschweig-Lüneburg-Celle. Both of these adopted primogeniture in the second half of the seventeenth century, but again, the basic division persisted.

The Hohenzollerns in Brandenburg had made a start toward primogeniture with the so-called *Constitutio Achillea* of 1473. Named after its creator, Elector Albert III Achilles (1414–1486), the statute left the Hohenzollern possessions as a whole divisible, though the march of Brandenburg itself was exempt. Interestingly, the elector referred to his entire arrangement as a "division." His immediate heirs, and even more remote ones, chose to ignore his strictures. Even as he admitted that the *Constitutio* had been useful, Elector Joachim I (1499–1535) split the government of Brandenburg between his two sons Joachim II (1505–1571) and John of Küstrin (1513–1571). Since both of these died in the same year, the new elector, John George (1525–1598), controlled all of the lands of the margravate. However, if his testament had stood, the territories would have been partitioned again. Instead, his firstborn, Elector Joachim Frederick (1546–1608), refused to accept this provision. He and the dwindling Franconian branch of the house came to an agreement in 1599, which was subsequently widened in 1603. Under its terms, to the primary electoral branch of the house and its firstborn male would go the *Kurmark* along with the *Neumark*. Should the Hohenzollern line of dukes die out in Prussia, as occurred in 1618, this province would fall to the electoral line as well. These provisions also applied to the early seventeenth-century acquisitions of Cleves, Mark, and Ravensburg in the Rhineland.

The Bavarian Wittelsbachs had agreed to especially crippling territorial divisions in the fourteenth century. By the beginning of the sixteenth century, almost all of the significant lines had died out, leaving the Munich branch with the lion's share of the dynasty's holdings. In 1506, Duke Albert IV of Bavaria-Munich (1447–1508) and his brother, Duke Wolfgang, resolved that primogeniture would be effective in their house from that time forward. Albert's second son, Ludwig, hotly contested the provision, however. The result was that from 1514 to 1545, the year of Ludwig's death, he and his oldest brother, Duke William IV (1493–1550), governed a large part of the Bavarian lands jointly. No formal division of their holdings took place however. William ordered that primogeniture be followed, as did his son, Albert V (1528–1579). Thus, from the second half of the sixteenth century, the Wittelsbachs followed the rule of the firstborn relatively strictly. Where younger brothers did establish hereditary lines in territories under their control, such as in the county of Leuchtenberg or in the Palatine-Neuburg, these lands either came to them through their wives or were insignificant parts of the Bavarian patrimony, which Munich in any case watched closely.

The imperial Habsburgs repeated the Wittelsbach pattern of family patrimony. Also divided several times in the fourteenth century, the totality of the Austrian lands were united once again only under Emperor Maximilian I (1459–1519) at the end of the fifteenth century. His grandson, Emperor Ferdinand I (1503–1564), who controlled the Austrian lands, divided them along with his newly won kingdoms of Hungary and Bohemia among his three sons at his death. Falling heir to all of the Habsburg territories by an agreement made among his uncles, Emperor Ferdinand II (1578–1637) declared primogeniture to be the rule of his house in 1635, although he had been forced to create a secundogeniture for his brother, Archduke Leopold, in the Tyrol. By the last third of the seventeenth century, the latter line no longer had any male heirs. From that time on, the Vienna branch controlled all of the Habsburg holdings.

Particularly complex were the divisions that took place in the house of Hesse. Philip the Magnanimous (1509–1567), who was to achieve notoriety for his bigamous second marriage, inherited the

Hessian lands intact from his father, Landgrave William II. Philip apportioned his lands among the four legitimate sons from his first marriage, although unequally. Of these divisions—Hesse-Kassel, Hesse-Darmstadt, and Hesse-Rheinfels—the first two endured through the nineteenth century. Hesse-Darmstadt introduced primogeniture in 1606, and Landgrave William IV of Hesse-Kassel mandated it in his testament at approximately the same time. Neither provision was fully effective, particularly in Hesse-Kassel. Here special lines were created in Phillippsthal and Rothenburg that lasted to the beginning of the eighteenth century. As late as 1862, the main branch of the house in Hesse-Kassel thought it advisable to reconfirm the primogeniture order in its house statutes. Darmstadt was less fragmented, though a special line of that house created in Homburg in the seventeenth century was a long-lasting source of trouble.

But for both the number of divisions and the tenacity with which they continued to make them, few German princes could match the record of the Wettin dukes of Saxony. The primary division, which then spawned many more, took place in 1485. This created the Ernestine, or electoral, line of the house, and the Albertine, or ducal, branch. Control of these lands and titles was reversed as a result of the Schmalkaldic Wars of 1547 in which Duke Maurice (1521–1553) fought on the side of the victorious Emperor Charles V, and Elector John Frederick (1503–1554) was the loser. As reward for the first and punishment for the latter, Charles turned the Albertines henceforth into electors and the Ernestines into dukes. The Albertines had adopted a form of primogeniture in 1499 and continued to observe this practice but not consistently. In 1652, however, Elector John George I (1585–1656) established from his private holdings three secondary lines for his heirs—Saxony-Weissenfels, Saxony-Merseburg, and Saxony-Zeitz—which sparked repeated quarrels in the house. The lands were not fully united again until 1746 after which primogeniture was closely observed in the line.

The ducal Ernestines, on the other hand, divided and redivided their lands several times in the latter third of the sixteenth century. By about 1600 two basic branches had appeared—Saxony-Weimar and Saxony-Gotha. These gave rise to eleven further divisions—four from Saxony-Weimar and seven from Saxony-Gotha. By the beginning of the eighteenth century, almost all of Saxony-Weimar's branches had died out, making it possible for Duke Ernest August (1688–1748) to introduce primogeniture in that branch of the house through his testament of 1717. Saxony-Gotha remained divided. By 1710, three lines—Saxony-Coburg, Saxony-Eisenberg, and Saxony-Römhild—had been redistributed among the four that remained. Saxony-Gotha-Altenburg adopted primogeniture in 1685, Saxony-Gotha-Hildburghausen in 1703, and Saxony-Gotha-Coburg in 1746. Saxony-Gotha-Meiningen dropped partible inheritance in 1802, just in time to win the emperor's permission for the step before Napoleon ended the old empire forever.[10]

These examples are drawn from the history of major German houses. They typify, however, what went on almost without exception among all German princely dynasties large and small—Baden, Mecklenburg, Waldeck, Reuss, and Schwarzburg, to name a few—down to the eighteenth century.

The drawbacks to partible inheritance seem many, the advantages few. Indeed, from our contemporary perspective, it would be hard to find anything politically or economically positive in the practice. It did, of course, bring with it certain long-term cultural advantages. University professors and musicians certainly benefited from wider employment opportunities fostered by the decentralization of intellectual and artistic life. All three of the courts operated by Ferdinand I's sons in Vienna, Innsbruck, and Graz became significant musical centers. Johann Sebastian Bach could look to Anhalt-Cöthen for employment when Saxony-Weimar proved not to his liking. But from an administrative point of view, about the only benefit of partible inheritance was the exercise it gave German bureaucrats in handling complex fractions. In the division of Meiningen between the Ernestine and Albertine Saxons in 1660, the portions for members of the two lines were reckoned in twelfths. The dukes of Saxony-Weimar and Saxony-Gotha then further divided the 7/24 of the administrative district (*Amt*) and city they jointly received.[11]

And yet, close examination suggests several reasons why the custom endured long beyond the Middle Ages. It solved certain practical problems. If a dynasty's holdings were extensive, partible inheritance was a way of keeping their administration within the family. The Habsburgs, for example, thought in these terms.[12] Land divisions were also a way to reward filial loyalty. According to Veit Ludwig von Seckendorff, whose *Teutscher Fürstenstaat* went through eight editions by 1720 and was perhaps the most authoritative commentary on German princely government of the day, rulers often came to such ideas as they reached advanced age.[13]

Territorial divisions were considered a way of keeping peace among the male members of a dynasty. Maurice of Hesse-Kassel (1572–1632) worried in 1620 that allowing one of his sons "sole supremacy" (*allainiger superioritet*) in his lands would provoke his younger brothers into banding against him with the knights in their territories as allies.[14] Germany's princes sometimes used the cause of unjustly treated younger sons as pretexts for armed attacks. The sixteenth-century Protestant Schmalkaldic League rationalized its offensive against the still-Catholic Duke Henry Julius the Younger of Braunschweig-Wolfenbüttel in 1541 in retaliation for the duke's alleged misuse of the inheritance of his younger brother, Duke William. When Landgrave Ernest of Hesse-Rheinfels-Rothenburg proposed in 1653 at the Diet of Regensburg that primogeniture be made the rule in all the empire's principalities, he also suggested that those who supported the idea consolidate in the event that other rulers attack them for their views.[15]

Younger sons found partible inheritance personally advantageous; others continued to think that it furthered their political interests. Representative bodies generally had a strong financial stake in preserving territorial integrity. Occasionally, however, they found divided patrimonies useful in efforts to curb princely power. When Albert IV of Bavaria died in 1508, his eldest son, the future Duke William IV, was still a minor. The Bavarian estates led the opposition to the late duke's will, which ordered that the rule of primogeniture be followed. Calling it a step toward monarchical dominance of all Bavarian subjects, they asked that William conduct his government with his brother, Ludwig, as mentioned above. The estates of the Tyrol welcomed the division of the Habsburg lands in the second half of the sixteenth century. Weary of being treated as only a part of a much larger whole by Emperors Maximilian I and Ferdinand I, they hoped that a resident *Landesherrscher*—in this case, Archduke Ferdinand II (1529–1595)—would be more attentive to their particular and traditional interests.[16]

Princes themselves continued to believe in many cases that partible inheritance would enhance their political power, especially in the imperial diet. Until almost the end of the sixteenth century, all those with some sort of independent territorial jurisdiction could vote in the appropriate college of that body. That some might be members of the same dynasty made no difference until 1654 when the multiplication of princely votes through territorial division really ceased. By simply increasing their own cohort, the secular princes hoped to weaken the influence of their more numerous spiritual colleagues. In this spirit, according to the eighteenth-century jurist John Jacob Moser, they mistakenly read a recess of the diet in 1570. This called for strengthening the empire, a mandate that the princes took to mean increasing their number of voting voices, not acquiring more lands and peoples.[17] If, indeed, this was their goal, they fulfilled it. In the thirteenth century there were around ninety spiritual princes and only thirteen secular ones. A hundred years later, the second group had grown to a little more than forty. By 1582 it numbered forty-six, a figure made even more impressive in light of the territorial losses that secularization in the name of Protestant reform had brought to the spiritual principalities.[18]

To a certain extent, the steadfast refusal of German princes and sometimes their consorts to accept primogeniture was rooted in the normal concern of all parents for the welfare of their children. When the lives and livelihoods of their offspring were at stake, rulers and their wives often gave vent to their deepest paternal and maternal feelings. Especially eloquent was the late sixteenth-century prince-dramatist Duke Henry Julius of Braunschweig-Wolfenbüttel. His blood-drenched play, "Von einem ungeratenen Sohn," revolves around a young prince who slaughters most of his family in order to rule their territories. His older brother, the heir and a good and decent man, comes upon his murdered son, Innocens. His anguished reaction says much about what at least one prince thought of parenthood: "O poor Innocens, oh you my dear guiltless son. What sort of a merciless spirit could it have been to have laid its hands on you? No lion, no dog, could have done it, for they are far too magnanimous to have attacked a defenseless thing. A dumb beast, a swine, a fowl, fights for its young, and would rather die itself than have something happen to them."[19]

As the source of their children's worldly goods, fathers had an awesome power, which obliged them, however, to provide for their offspring. During an age in which land and wealth were more often than not synonymous, partible inheritance was an obvious way to fulfill one's duties as a parent. If fathers temporarily forgot this responsibility, sons, especially younger ones, were always ready to remind them of it. Christian Henry of Braunschweig-Hannover did just that in 1685, arguing that a parent could justly divide his inheritance unequally only if a child plotted against his life. Even such outright opponents of partible inheritance as William IV of Hesse-Kassel and August II the Strong (1670–1733), elector of Saxony and king of Poland, continued funding the pretentions of junior members in their houses, irksome though they found the obligation to be.[20]

The widows of princes ordinarily drew their pensions from their husband's possessions. It was thus imperative that a young man have lands of his own in order to marry advantageously.[21] Lacking the means to keep even a household appropriate to his station, a prince might not marry at all and possibly turn to soldiering as a career. The hazards of this occupation did not respect niceties of rank. European ruling houses saw a sharp rise in the number of family members lost in combat during the seventeenth century. The increase among those fallen was borne entirely by the bachelors among them.[22] German rulers therefore had every reason to spare their sons a military life. Those who forced their male children into this profession through the introduction of primogeniture stood accused in the eyes of many of their contemporaries. Elector Ernest August of Braunschweig-Hannover (1629–1698), who brought the rule of the firstborn to his lands in 1683, had two younger sons die in imperial service. "In such a fashion has the duke of Hannover, your master, sacrificed two of his sons," commented one of Ernest August's princely colleagues to the elector's librarian and advisor, Gottfried William von Leibniz.[23]

Princesses were just as protective of their children's rights as were fathers, if not more so. Few went so far as the loving Rebecca, in Hans Sachs's sixteenth-century "Jacob," who substituted a beloved younger son for the elder when the time for the paternal blessing came, but many were close in spirit to their Old Testament counterpart. The introduction of primogeniture in Hannover was especially embittered by the strong affection that Duchess Sophia bore for her second son, Prince Frederick August.[24] Second wives were especially tenacious in guarding the interests of their own issue. A seventeenth-century countess of Reuss did her best to overturn a house primogeniture statute of 1668, which favored the eldest son from the first marriage of her husband, Count Henry I.[25] Juliana of Nassau-Siegen, the second wife of Landgrave Maurice the Learned of Hesse-Kassel (1572–1632), was instrumental in persuading her husband to divide his inheritance more equitably among the offspring of his two marriages. Comparing copies of Maurice's first will, done in 1608 for the children of his first wife, with the third, drawn up in 1620 (with Juliana's offspring in mind), one can see how much his resolve to introduce a form of primogeniture in his house had weakened. The first document spoke clearly of his firstborn son as his "universal heir." The last testament, addressed to the four sons of his second marriage, markedly softened this.[26] The blandishments of his second wife may in part have led the otherwise unsentimental Elector Frederick William the Great Elector of Brandenburg to thrust primogeniture aside in his testament of 1686. Because of the death of his oldest son, however, and the opposition to partible inheritance of his successor, the future King Frederick I (1657–1713), the provision never became effective.[27]

Nor did princesses confine their appeals to rulers when the welfare of their children was at stake. Relying upon the shared sympathies of nurturers, they acted on a woman-to-woman basis as well. When Elector August (1526–1586) of Saxony became the guardian of the sons of his cousin, Duke John William of Saxony-Weimar (1530–1573), he decided to change the boys' tutors. Upset at the impact this might have on her youngsters, their mother, Duchess Dorothy Susanna, turned not only to the elector but to his wife, Electress Anna, as well. The duchess begged her counterpart to remember that "we carried our beloved son for nine months under our heart." She hoped that, understanding the suffering caused by "such motherly concerns," Anna would intercede on her behalf with her husband.[28]

The right of any woman to make this claim did not stem from the maternal relationship alone. These were the wives of princes who, by the sixteenth century, were almost always equal in birth to their husbands. Their status defined the rank of a child as much as did that of their male partners. Some women therefore took any effort to reduce the territorial position of any of their sons as an affront to their own reputations. Perhaps the most notable example of this attitude was found in the person of Kunigunde of Austria, the sister of Maximilian I and wife of Albert IV of Bavaria. She was not a signatory to her husband's primogeniture decree. Rather, she denounced it altogether following his death.[29] Her reasons for doing so, given to an imperial commission sent to investigate the dispute, spoke tellingly of a mother's contribution to the status of her son: "I am born a princess of Austria, and have married a prince of Bavaria, and through him I have received young princes, not counts or bastards; for him [her second son, Duke Ludwig] to be scorned and held as one [a count or a bastard] . . . that I cannot suffer."[30]

In asking the emperor to work out some sort of agreement between Ludwig and his elder brother William, Kunigunde made it clear that it was a question of protecting her own "maternal dignity and honor" (*"Muetter Wirden und Eern"*) Her "wifely honor and authority" required that the exclusive rule of her *primogenitus* be overturned. She was sure that had her husband lived long enough, he too would have changed his views.[31]

Kunigunde's stress on the importance of her status in the bloodlines of her sons points us to the most significant reason for the persistence of primogeniture in Germany. It reinforced—indeed, played a major functional role—in the dynastic system that governed so many German territories. The belief that a ruling family's patrimony and its polity were in some way the same was not confined to the German houses of Europe.[32] Nor was the nature of that relationship altogether clear. The question of whether the proprietary rights of the dynasty extended to the totality of a principality or to only part of it, whether ownership, if any, was direct or indirect, remained at issue until European republicanism swept the question aside in more modern times. But, imperfect as the definition of these concepts was, almost all princes prior to the end of the eighteenth century subscribed to some variant of the proposition that the lands they governed belonged to their families. Thus, they had extensive rights over their disposal.

Partible inheritance was not absolutely necessary for dynastic rule to operate. The Norman-Plantagenet and Capetian kingships were not notably impaired by primogeniture. Neither Germanic nor Roman law says anything about the rule of the firstborn. A distinguished eighteenth-century German commentator on the practice, George Melchior Ludolf, professed to find it in the Mosaic Code and German custom, but he was speaking here far more as a partisan than as a detached student of the subject.[33] That primogeniture should have flourished in France and England and not in Germany must be attributable to the peculiar historical circumstances of the latter. It should be noted, however, that the premise that a territorial inheritance belongs to a dynasty collectively gives rise syllogistically to the conclusion that all members of that house are entitled to a part of that inheritance. Duke George of Braunschweig-Lüneburg described his sons as "brothers of one princely house and likewise of one body." Elector Frederick III of the Palatinate believed the same thing, calling his branch of the Wittelsbachs part of a "stem." From this he drew the territorial corollary that all its members were entitled to a part of its holdings.[34] For the female, this share came in her dowry and other wedding gifts from her house. For the male, it meant that he had the right to govern his family's lands, however these were defined, and to draw revenues from them.[35] Even after the sons of Emperor Maximilian II (1527–1576) renounced outright division of the Habsburg Austrian patrimony, they continued to insist on their rights as princes to participate in the administration of these territories. Thus, in 1585, upon the death of the governor of Austria above the Enns,

Archduke Matthias asked his brother, Emperor Rudolf II (1552–1612), to confer responsibility for the area on him "because [the administration] was earlier also carried out by princely persons of our illustrious house."[36]

To judge by their testaments, many of Germany's princes preferred that their sons rule their dynasty's lands jointly. Partition was recommended only should collective government prove unworkable. These were the prescriptions of Landgrave Philip of Hesse's will of 1562. Clearly worried about the economic and military disadvantages of splitting his holdings, Ernest the Pious of Saxony-Weimar-Gotha (1601–1675) urged his sons to govern their inheritance together. Even when princes did give their offspring separate shares of their patrimony, they continued to exact some concession to the unity of those lands from their subjects or from their legatees themselves. The former were often asked to swear fealty to all ruling brothers; the latter sometimes paid each other a small sum to underscore the essential oneness of their patrimony.[37]

Thus, partible inheritance was one way of expressing the role of the dynasty as a whole in its lands. Lines of inheritance were seen to move laterally through entire generations rather than vertically through succeeding ones. John William, duke of Saxony-Weimar, claimed rights in the Saxony-Gotha of his banned brother as his sibling and nearest agnate. Elector Frederick III of the Palatinate saw merit in his contention, calling the brothers "common heirs and territorial princes."[38] Following the death of Emperor Maximilian I in 1519, Mercurino Gattinara, Charles V's chancellor, told the Austrian estates that it made little difference who ruled them—the new Emperor Charles V or his brother Ferdinand. Nor should there be any concern about whether the young men ruled the Habsburg patrimony jointly or separately.[39]

So powerful was the notion that a dynasty's holdings were a collective possession that it acted as a brake on the emperor's right to punish a disobedient vassal through confiscation. By fortifying his lands against Maximilian II in a conspiracy to reestablish the Ernestines in the electoral line, John Frederick of Saxony-Gotha theoretically forfeited them to his sovereign. Once he captured the duke, however,

Maximilian was willing to divide his prisoner's lands among his sons. Indeed, so concerned was the Habsburg that the boys receive justice in the Wettin holdings as a whole that he ordered their uncle, Duke John William, to pay them additional compensation should he become the Elector of Saxony.[40] Nor was the emperor alone in his belief that the collective right of a house to its lands had to be observed. Individual princely fathers often saw their power over their children challenged on this point. The drawn-out dispute in seventeenth-century Hesse-Kassel over the will of Landgrave Maurice hung on the question of whether or not a parent could introduce primogeniture, which minimized the joint nature of inheritance, simply because he wished to do so.[41]

Closely tied to the idea of dynastic possessions as collective familial possessions was that of the equality of all legitimately born princes in any given house. Both her sons, said Kunigunde of Austria, were born to her in wedlock, thus ruling out inequalities of inheritance or title.[42] Even families embroiled in long-standing territorial disputes among themselves stressed the equality of males within the order.[43] The constitutional structure of the empire further reinforced the idea. All male members of a princely family were *reichsunmittelbar*. Changes in inheritance practices had to come through mutual agreement in the house. If these were made among brothers, imperial confirmation, though desirable, was not necessary. If a father reworked these provisions for his offspring in his own will, however, then the emperor had to give his assent. If possible, it was also wise to have the approval of the imperial Diet. Traditionally, all princes of a given house received the regalia to their lands collectively, "a true *feudum genearchium*," as a councillor of Anhalt boasted.[44] When a family member felt that any of his siblings was trying to violate this, extended protests followed. As Christian II of Anhalt-Bernburg (1599–1656) put it, there was no such thing as partial participation in one's imperial princely dignity.[45]

Princely equality had to be served in territorial divisions and the settlement of disputes over them. All other goals receded before this one. In the bitter Saxon land dispute of the 1570s over the territories of the imprisoned Duke John Frederick, Emperor Maximilian II was advised that he should proceed according to the dictates of justice and "due equality" (*billichmassige gleichheit*). This meant, among other things that "district against district, value against value, each and every quality and circumstance against one another, [all] should be measured, compensated for and equalized."[46] The appearance of inequality in princely territorial partitions was scrupulously avoided, or, if that were impossible, carefully masked. Defending Duke John William of Saxony-Weimar's claims against his brother's sons in the Saxon division, his ambassador, Hans Rosbeck, protested that his lord wanted no "undue advantage." Rather, all that he wished was to have equality maintained. On the other hand, Elector August, the boys' guardian, denied that the duke had any concern about the issue at all. He argued that the four districts that John William wished to obtain from a redivision would give him as much income as he drew from Weimar alone. Such an arrangement would, in the elector's opinion, have left John Frederick's sons at a great disadvantage.[47]

Those who investigated these cases were as solicitous of the equality of princes as those who brought them. The imperial commission advising Maximilian II in the Saxon suit resolved that no one would knowingly be awarded less than was due him and that equality would be observed as much as possible. The emperor himself echoed these sentiments and hoped that future misunderstandings could be avoided through adherence to such guidelines.[48]

Primogeniture, in the eyes of many German princes, undermined these values, indeed, destroyed them altogether. It was "the rule of a single territorial prince and unequal division of the land," as a pact introducing the practice in Hesse-Kassel noted in 1654.[49] It brought "trouble, unfairness, and inequality," noted the councillors of the house of Anhalt in 1635.[50] The practice excluded all but the firstborn from having a voice in important affairs, as Albert of Saxony-Gotha (1648–1699) pointed out in 1678, whereas the normal custom in his house was to decide matters through a form of princely majority rule.[51]

Brothers resented losing even a consultative voice when primogeniture was adopted.[52] Worst of all, primogeniture forever excluded some family members from any serious administrative and political life of their own, utterly negating the idea that "the splendor of the house should also appear in me," a belief that Maximilian William of Braunschweig-Hannover and countless other young German princes cherished.[53] Having the sanction of long family tradition made partible inheritance even more acceptable. Kunigunde of Austria was clearly twisting fact to her own purposes when at the beginning of the sixteenth century she called primogeniture "unheard of" in the German lands.[54] Nevertheless, during an age in which innovation was not an end in itself, princes and their advisors took obvious satisfaction in following the customs of their progenitors when observing divided and equal inheritances.

Thus, partible inheritance had deep and sturdy roots in German constitutional theory, political usage, and even in the human heart. Whatever disadvantages it brought with it were substantially offset by all or some of the above considerations as late as the latter part of the seventeenth century. But none of our discussion thus far explains two developments crucial to our story. One is that the marked upturn of interest in primogeniture among German princes at the turn of the sixteenth century was not sustained. The second is that the greatest number of territorial divisions took place from roughly 1550 to 1650. This was true of the Ernestine Saxons, for example, who effected the greatest number of new partitions during this time, although only Gotha, along with its Coburg and Meiningen lines, had full imperial representation.[55] That all of this coincided with the appearance of the Protestant Reformation and its spread in Germany raises a reasonable possibility that religious concerns may, in some way, have retarded the adoption of the rule of the firstborn, thereby actually impeding the consolidation of German princely power. To explore this hypothesis fully, we must move from the realm of the utilitarian to that of the spirit, a leap that institutional history does not always negotiate comfortably. But the Reformation was, if nothing else, an era of heightened religiosity among all elements of society, princes included. And the confessional upheavals of the day may have influenced their treatment of, and attitude toward, their offspring.

John Jacob Moser, who published the first volume of his *Teutsches Staatsrecht* in 1737 and was therefore still very close to the scene, maintained that religious belief did indeed retard primogeniture in Germany. While he gave due attention to the political, personal, and economic concerns already mentioned, he stressed another: "Some pious princes (who at that time still had immeasureably greater respect for the Bible than most of today's do) held that it [primogeniture] was directly against the word of God, according to which children of the same father should have equal shares of his legacy."[56] A self-styled "German and Imperial Patriot" had said much the same thing at the very beginning of the eighteenth century: "Our ancestors accustomed themselves only with difficulty to a privilege which they believed to be incompatible with the equality of love which religion required of fathers for all their children, and this . . . did not find partisans and approval easily."[57]

Modern scholars have concurred, though there were cases in which the attitude was more tactical than otherworldly.[58] German rulers, Protestants and Catholics alike, in the sixteenth and seventeenth centuries were religious as well as secular politicians, responsible for the perpetuation of their faith and the survival of its institutions. Throughout the sixteenth century, territorial subdivisions multiplied the number of reformed princes in the diet dramatically. Defections from their faith were serious matters, particularly when they occurred within their own dynasties. The rewards of inheritance were frequently used to keep waverers within the church of their house. In his will of 1595 Landgrave Ludwig of Hesse-Marburg (1537–1604) ordered his heirs to keep to the true confession on pain of losing the lands assigned to them.[59]

But deeply moral and spiritual considerations also persuaded the German princes to continue partible inheritance. They were not unique in their feelings. For example, as sentimental ties of parents to their offspring grew in late seventeenth- and eighteenth-century France, so too did the feeling that children deserved equal affection from their elders. The result was heavy criticism of primogeniture from educators and philosophers alike and the temporary abolition of the custom during the Revolution.[60]

Both public and private documents make it plain that religious considerations weighed heavily in the minds of sixteenth- and seventeenth-century German princes when they distributed their holdings among their children. Moved either by the Protestant reform or its Catholic counterpart, many rulers were far more mindful of scripture and pastoral teaching than either their predecessors or successors. This attitude was not confined to matters of inheritance. Secular and religious concerns were closely intertwined wherever one looks in the sixteenth century.[61] But nowhere do we see this more clearly than in princely testaments, which were marked by heightened religiosity in both the personal and institutional sense of that term.

As a civil instrument, a prince's will was central to the function of dynastic government. It guided and bound a house's territorial organization almost absolutely. Only the emperor could break its provisions, and many legal hurdles stood in the way of those who tried to do so. The testament strictly enjoined future generations to fulfill the wishes of a forebear. The inflexibility of these documents was burdensome to many, but few circumvented them. If they did, princes risked serious challenges to their testamentary authority within their own families. Frederick August of Braunschweig-Hannover protested his father's introduction of primogeniture in their house on the ground that the wills of their ancestors had not mandated the custom. His grandfather, Duke George of Braunschweig-Calenberg (1582–1641) had divided his lands among his sons, one of them Frederick August's father, Ernest August. In doing so, the duke had observed that the rule of the firstborn had never obtained in the line. Such being the case, Frederick August could see no reason to obey his father when the latter was not obeying his![62]

Italian testaments of the late Middle Ages often exhorted a *paterfamilias* to order his household so as to avoid "quarrels and disputes" among his heirs. Confronting their mortality in the sixteenth and seventeenth centuries, Germany's princes reworked this originally secular formula into a religious and moral imperative. Often they did so on the advice of spiritual leaders. Thus, Luther's sermon on dying advised men to draw up wills so as to forestall discord among those left behind; Wolfgang of Anhalt-Cöthen-Bernburg incorporated a good portion of that text into his own testament.[63] Indeed, one measure of the theological significance that German rulers read into their wills was the amount of space in them devoted to religious matters. Such concerns had cropped up in the testaments of their forebears, but these were usually limited to routine assertions of belief and commendations of the soul to God. In the sixteenth and seventeenth centuries, Protestant and Catholic alike used these documents for detailed confessional statements. Paragraph after paragraph urged heirs to remain loyal to the true faith, however that was seen, and made elaborate provision to further the church and Christian education. Lengthy excerpts from doctrinal summaries such as the Augsburg Confession or the late sixteenth-century Lutheran Formula of Concord replaced perfunctory biblical citations.[64]

Thus the princely testament, always central to the dynastic constitution, had become a vehicle to express piety and to soften the wrath of one's Maker. Intrafamilial property arrangements were transposed into Christian didactic paradigms. Duke George of Braunschweig-Calenberg believed in 1541 that by making a testament, one avoided God's punishment and curse.[65] Both divine and parental wills were at work when inheritances were established for children, noted a group of advisors at the very Catholic court of Archduke Charles of Styria late in the sixteenth century.[66] Bemoaning the moral decline of the empire's princes, Ernest the Pious of Saxony-Gotha, *"Beternst"* to cynical contemporaries, hoped that his testament would establish guidelines to keep his heirs straight in their ways.[67]

Lutherans in general stressed the family as a teaching arm of the faith; the princely testament performed that function in the most complex set of household relations that the age knew. A valuable spiritual lesson was to be learned even from the sometimes arbitrary divisions of territory to which siblings submitted. In his *Der ander Teil Promptuarii exemplorum, darinnen viel herrliche schöne Historien . . . und Exempel von Tugend und Untugend . . . verfaset sind,* Zacharias Rivander, a sixteenth-century Lutheran moralist, pointed approvingly to the behavior of the eldest son of the fourteenth-century Margrave Frederick of Brandenburg (1287–1332), Prince Johann (d. 1357).

Passed over in the order of succession, the young man dutifully accepted the decision of his sire, trusting to the better judgment of his elders.[68]

Thus a ruler's testament offered a kind of practicum in the Fifth Commandment for the young of high station. But Scripture spoke to more than parental rights. It said something about duties as well, in particular about treating one's heirs equally. For Germany's Reformation rulers, the disposition of land was not only a political and economic act, but a religious and moral one as well. Indeed, it was often impossible to tell one from the other. Elector Frederick of the Palatinate and others were fond of quoting the biblical injunction that a divided house could not stand, by which he meant a dynasty torn by dissent, not by the territorial divisions designed to mute such hostilities.[69]

Many princes of sixteenth- and seventeenth-century Germany therefore passed their dynastic holdings either collectively or already divided to their heirs with an eye both to the world beyond as well as the one at hand. Though this was as true of Catholics as it was of Protestants, Luther seems to have had an especially strong impact on his princely followers when it came to this question. "Since we are children we are also heirs" (Romans 8:17) was one influential passage. Duke Wolfgang of the Palatinate-Zweibrücken (1526–1569) took his guidance from *Ecclesiasticus,* a book that the Wittenberg reformer especially recommended to heads of households. Thus, the biblical command "When the end comes, and you must take your leave, then divide your inheritance" prompted Wolfgang and others to do just that, as freely as they wished. John William of Saxony-Weimar regarded partible inheritance as the will of God. That the practice had long obtained among German princes lent further support to this argument.[70]

Religious precept associated with partible inheritance also reinforced the ideals of brotherly equality advanced by German princes throughout the Middle Ages. Evaluating this last-named principle in the light of Scripture, John William of Saxony-Weimar was sure that it had "the blessing of God." In Austria, Archdukes Charles and Leopold urged their brother, Emperor Ferdinand II, to get on with the division of the Habsburg patrimony, calling the equality they expected him to respect pleasing to the Almighty.[71] Christian of Anhalt-Bernburg ordered that even new fiefs his sons might acquire be equally divided among them, "not doubting that through such means they will have the blessings of God."[72] Ernest the Pious of Saxony-Gotha recommended in his testament of 1654 that the eldest of his sons direct the affairs of the house and be properly compensated for it. Otherwise, the brothers were to treat one another as equals. If they should decide to divide the lands that had been passed on to them collectively, none among them was to be either favored or disadvantaged. Citing the testament of John William of Saxony-Weimar, Ernest urged his heirs to strive for "Christian and just equality."[73]

Princes often preferred that sibling equality be expressed through a commonly shared government of one with the eldest son as director— the so-called *Seniorat*. Yet, where this arrangement was called for, either through paternal testament or agreement among brothers, elaborate conditions were set to keep any prince from dominating the group. Consultation and collective decisions among all concerned were encouraged so that, as the princes of Anhalt said in 1635, "no one would have to forego his princely estate, grandeur, dignity, and rank."[74] The lands of Saxony-Gotha, for example, were handled this way for a short time beginning in 1629. As the eldest of four brothers, Duke William (1598–1662) was charged for a period of six years with conducting foreign and major domestic affairs of his house. This responsibility gave him claim to certain honors and dignities his siblings did not enjoy. He chaired meetings with his brothers and could speak before any of them. Beyond this, however, all had a voice in dynastic matters. Majority votes among them decided mutual concerns, including administration of the hunting preserves of the house. All brothers could visit the treasury, council rooms, and consistory, the governing body of the Lutheran church, as often as they wished. The court was to be maintained in common, and each prince was assigned an income from the various lands of the house. Some legal authorities believed that this arrangement was closer to the spirit of princely equality than other schemes.[75]

But many rulers and jurists were not altogether sure how to distinguish the *Seniorat* from primogeniture. The confusion and outright hostility that ensued often made outright territorial division necessary.[76] The problems in the Saxony-Gotha of Duke William and his brothers were typical of many houses. Disputes among the duke and his brothers ranged from the precise nature of William's administrative authority to the question of who controlled new lands that fell to Saxony-Gotha as years went by. The single court was a catastrophe. Not only was it excessively large and costly, but household personnel often did not know whether they served the dynasty as a whole or only a member of it. This problem grew more acute when princes married.[77]

Viewed in twentieth-century perspective, the division of a dynasty's lands under such circumstances was a setback for dynastic collectivism. Filled with a high sense of moral and religious purpose, most contemporary princes did not see it that way at all. Indeed, they celebrated their decisions to split their patrimony and read into their agreements all of the spiritual values that their fathers did when they partitioned a family's lands among their male heirs in their testaments. The final purpose of these pacts was fraternal unity that conferred upon them the blessings of God, at least in the eyes of the princes of Anhalt in 1603. One of their predecessors, Prince Bernard (1540–1570), had composed a prayer in 1568 that equated the love of God for man and His concern for him with brotherly loyalty and affection.[78]

To be sure, not all territorial divisions among brothers took place under such high-toned auspices. The three surviving sons of Duke George of Braunschweig-Calenberg do not seem to have required the power of prayer in 1665 to iron out what they thought were mere confusions in the text of their father's will.[79] Far more typical, however, were princes who rejoiced, as they partitioned their family's holdings, over the Christian equality they were about to establish. The tone was strikingly different from pre-Reformation arrangements of this kind. For example, Duke Albert and Elector Ernest of Saxony in 1485 believed that they had reached a just and friendly agreement with the help of God, but no further sermonizing seemed necessary. August of Anhalt-Zerbst (1575–1653) was far more expansive in

1636. A pact that he had closed with his brothers was based in "God's word, good conscience, tradition, contemporary practice among other princely houses, and the general welfare."[80] In 1641 Ernest the Pious of Saxony-Gotha soared to heights of lyric eloquence on the subject. Receiving the oath of fealty from lands awarded him in a territorial division with his brothers, he described to those present how princes received their mandate. Some were chosen directly by God—Saul and David for example. Others came to their position through territorial partition, either through lot or "through good and friendly agreement; here God also is acting who furthers his gracious works that brothers are in harmony with one another and agree among themselves without quarreling or discord, one yielding to the right, the other to the left; who [God] guides their hearts like flowing waters creating peace at their boundaries, so that each one is content with his district and the land and peoples allotted to him."[81]

The devoutly Lutheran Saxon was here apostrophizing not only the results of such negotiations but the process itself. Others did the same. Prince Ludwig of Anhalt-Cöthen (1579–1650) believed so fervently in the moral significance of territorial discussions among his brothers that he composed his memoirs of them. He was sure that God's hand was at work in these talks when the councillors through-out the Anhalt domains responded swiftly to queries about the impact of a projected partition.[82]

Thus, in the sixteenth and seventeenth centuries fraternal equality became not only a dynastic norm but a religious duty as well. Inequality was therefore twice unacceptable. Philip of Hesse's conscience weighed heavily on him when he was confronted with the problem of favoring one son over all the others. This attitude of a typical princely father carried over to their sons. Division compacts among brothers took great care to assure posterity that no one among them had been disadvantaged, particularly the younger members of the house.[83]

Partible inheritance fit very comfortably into this way of thinking; primogeniture, only with great strain. To the very end of the seventeenth century, some German princes continued to reject the rule of the firstborn on religious grounds. The sons of Ernest the Pious of

Saxony-Gotha condemned the custom in the strongest terms possible in 1678. Following what they called "all-knowing God and our consciences," they accepted their oldest brother as their executive director but were happy that the interests of the youngest among them were well protected. The latter, they triumphantly proclaimed, "had nothing of their sovereign rights removed, suppressed or limited, but in every way true equality has been kept to the forefront and therefore nothing which smacks of the domination of a single individual, even less of the condition of primogeniture, crept in either directly or indirectly."[84] In 1662, the dukes of Weimar repeated an earlier agreement not to introduce primogeniture, which they described as "foreign, unequal, and unseemly, destructive in the highest of the princely estate and of the unity of brothers or cousins who are equally born."[85]

Religious considerations lay behind yet another motive to reject primogeniture. This was especially true among Protestants. Luther, who advised the princes of his faith on questions not only of Christian belief but of conduct of public life as well, consistently downplayed secular interests in patrimonial as well as in other disputes when asked for his counsel.[86] Urging Elector John Frederick and Duke Maurice of Saxony to abandon their quarrel over the bishopric of Wenzen in 1542, he argued that for all its wealth the territory was not worth the trouble. When quarrels over land arose among brothers, the devil was at work. The fiscal and strategic stakes that provoked these disputes were at best secondary considerations.[87] "Wood, stone, or land (*Raum*)" were an altogether different order of things from matters of conscience, as he pointed out to Count Albert of Mansfeld in a territorial disagreement with his brothers in 1525.[88]

One expects such views from a theologian and moralist. But practical men of politics took them to heart as well and used them, among other things, to justify partible inheritance. Reflecting in 1573 on those electoral houses that had adopted the practice, Duke John William of Saxony-Weimar suspected that they had done so only to enhance their earthly power.[89] There may have been a measure of sour grapes in these musings; John William was, at that moment, involved in a bitter territorial feud with Elector August of Saxony whose branch of the Wettin house did observe primogeniture. But there is no mistaking the religious ardor behind an anonymous denunciation of primogeniture in Weimar in 1675: "The introduction of primogeniture is done only with regard for external splendor . . . and does not show very much confidence in God."[90]

Relegating younger sons to the life of a landless *secundogenitus* often whetted those worldly ambitions deplored by devout Protestant princes. Even confessional loyalties suffered. The later career of Cardinal Frederick of Hesse is a good example. Though his saddened relatives in Hesse-Darmstadt tried to find more adequate incomes for the money- and prestige-hungry young man, none were commensurate to his self-image. Following his conversion to Catholicism in 1637, he went to Malta, became a knight, fought in twenty campaigns against the Turks, and finally became grand master of the order. The dreary existence of living on an allowance from his family had few attractions compared to, as he said, one in which he met nobility from all of Europe. He went out of his way to describe to the *primogenitus*, Landgrave George, how he had received his uniform and insignia from "the holy father" himself who had behaved in a most "fatherly" way toward him.[91] It was precisely this attitude, along with this set of consequences, that Lutheran and Calvinist princes hoped partible inheritance would forestall.

In such a way then did Germany's princes share the spiritual preoccupations of the sixteenth and seventeenth centuries and mold their policies accordingly. However, though these were religious concerns, they were not foreign to political practice. For polities in which dynastic government was the norm, dynastic values obtained. Partible inheritance fit very comfortably into this system. That they met religious precept further confirmed the practice and made it all the more worthy of respect. To change the system of inheritance a ruler had to make a decision that was both politically and religiously distasteful. The worst effects of divided inheritance could be mitigated by control of reproduction, of course—the fewer the offspring, the more concentrated the resources of the house would remain. But here too, dynastic and religious imperatives intertwined in a way that Protestant princes would find unexpectedly problematic.

CHAPTER II
"GOTT MACHT KINDER"

"God makes children," Luther observed; yet German princes were not always prepared to accommodate this blessing.[1] Too many children, particularly adult males, strained and sometimes even destroyed the resources of houses practicing partible inheritance. Imperatives that encouraged the overproduction of heirs therefore burdened the entire system. But having too few offspring conjured up problems more dangerous still. Children were the key to dynastic survival. Somewhere in the minds of kings and princes always lurked the fear that they would not have a legitimate male heir. The most august of establishments could be quickly wiped out if one generation was unfruitful or if death laid it waste. Emperor Leopold I (1640–1705) fell into near panic when he unexpectedly found himself the last male in the German branch of his line. By February 9, 1664, three Habsburg archdukes had died within fourteen months. Watching his last brother, Joseph, expire in 1665, Leopold noted that while one must yield to the will of God in such matters, it was nevertheless crucial for the house to reproduce itself as soon as possible.[2]

No one knew exactly how many sons were needed for a line to survive. Studies of mortality rates among the sixteenth- and seventeenth-century Swedish nobility have concluded that a house in which only three males reached maturity could afford to have only one remain single.[3] But statistical norms were not wholly reliable either, as the example of Leopold I reminds us. German princes in early modern Europe simply did not think in fixed figures when they estimated how many sons were needed to carry on succession within a dynasty. "Two, three, or as many as are alive," calculated Emperor Ferdinand II somewhat vaguely when advising a younger brother, Leopold, on the number of males the latter would have to sire in order for his line in the Tyrol to continue.[4]

German princes often hesitated to observe primogeniture because they feared that landless sons would remain bachelors, thereby reducing any future pool of eligible heirs. Maximilian I opposed the scheme of Albert IV of Bavaria to pass the entirety of his holdings to his oldest son, William, in part because he thought that the second son would not marry and thus would jeopardize the entire Wittelsbach patrimony. The emperor urged William's brother, Duke Ludwig, to take a wife and held out hope for a permanent territorial settlement in the lands of an unmarried uncle, Duke Wolfgang, when the latter died.[5] Philip of Hesse's refusal to disinherit his sons by his second, and bigamous, marriage may in part have stemmed from his fear that if he died without heirs, his lands would go to electoral Saxony. A pact between the two houses had provided for such an arrangement. One of the younger sons, Ludwig (from Philip's first union), married but after three years still had no children. Ludwig's eldest brother, William, refrained from taking a wife at all because of the expense involved, despite his father's entreaties to the contrary.[6] One of the considerations that prompted Frederick William the Great Elector to break the rule of primogeniture operative in his line since the end of the sixteenth century was that his younger son, who had received only a financial settlement from his father, might not marry at all. Since their forebears had never sired males in large numbers, the elector believed that leaving any of his issue bachelors risked extinguishing the Hohenzollerns in Brandenburg. Indeed, he had good reason to worry. Six years had passed between the death of his first son in 1649 and the birth of another, Karl Emil. A second prince, Frederick, was born, and then a third, Ludwig, who died within a year. As Frederick William drew up his testament in 1664, seeming to have no further prospects, he created a secundogeniture for Prince Frederick.[7]

Because of high infant mortality rates, Germany's princes were sincere in giving thanks to God for successful accouchements.[8] The wish of Count Gunther of Waldeck (1557–1585) that the Almighty would "one time" grant his wife a happy birth reflected many previous disappointments.[9] A new child was welcomed, regardless of sex, even when a difficult birth caused the death of a beloved spouse. One of the most successful dynastic matches of the sixteenth century—that of Emperor Ferdinand I and his Jagellonian wife, Anna of Hungary—ended sadly in 1547 when the latter died in Prague after being delivered of their fifteenth child. An anonymous verse, stitched together in the Bohemian capital, celebrated Anna's virtues and mourned her passing. However, the author pointedly absolved the baby, Archduchess Johanna, of any responsibility for her mother's fate:

> Her last royal child,
> By which the queen left this earth
> Is called Johanna, the high born.
> Exalted still in tender years,
> The little child is not to blame,
> She too, would have preferred
> To see her majesty, her dear mother.[10]

But the livelihoods of not only princes were at stake in the production of offspring. More humble folk had cause to rejoice in large ruling families as well. The preparation for the birth of a prince or princess demanded the skills of a variety of artisans to produce the necessary birthing bed, cradles, covers, mattresses, pillows, and curtains. If the

sketchy records of the court of Ferdinand I permit such generaliza-
tions, these appointments had to be supplied anew each time. Fur-
riers, drapers, not to mention carpenters, all found employment
through this single event.[11]

Because children were highly valued, it should surprise no one that
German princes produced many offspring if possible. Indeed, their
rate of reproduction could be staggering. Double-digit birthrates
were at times the rule rather than the exception. From the sixteenth to
the eighteenth centuries in the electoral and ducal lines of the Saxon
Wettins, two princes sired eleven heirs; four, twelve; one, fourteen;
two, fifteen; and two, eighteen and nineteen, respectively. The house
of Hesse performed in a like fashion. Three of Landgrave Philip's
descendants to the eighteenth century fathered seventeen, eighteen,
and nineteen offspring, respectively. Another brought forth fifteen
children, while others produced ten, twelve, fourteen, and fifteen.
Two had ten. Only four had fewer than seven offspring, and of those,
two fathered six.[12]

The only thing remarkable about these statistics, in view of the
need for princely heirs in any generation, is that this reproductive
rate, or at least the consistency of it, was peculiar to the sixteenth and
seventeenth centuries. From the thirteenth century to the beginning
of the sixteenth, the greatest number of children produced by a single
Wettin in any generation was nine, with seven being the most common number. The house of Hesse behaved much the same.

Good fortune marked the reproductive efforts of Germany's rulers
in other ways as well. Although the average life expectancy of a prince
both at birth and at age fifteen declined throughout Europe between
1500 and 1699, the overall number of those who survived beyond
ages fifteen, fifty, and seventy actually increased.[13] Philip of Hesse's
four sons from his first marriage all outlived him. Wolfgang of Pfalz-
Zweibrücken left five living male offspring when he died in 1569.
Furthermore, this situation repeated itself generation after generation. Up until the seventeenth century, only two sons among the
Saxon dukes had normally outlived their fathers. Duke John of Saxony-Weimar left four living when he died in 1605. His son Ernest the
Pious was outlived by seven! Such survival rates contrasted sharply

with earlier ones. Among the Wettins, one has to go back to Elector Frederick the Quarrelsome (1370–1428) to find someone who was outlived by four sons, all of them minors at that. The house of Hesse and the Wittelsbachs of the Palatinate had had similar experiences at the same time, not to be repeated until the sixteenth and seventeenth centuries.

Purely biological factors undoubtedly helped shape these figures. The close inbreeding of the Spanish and Austrian Habsburgs adversely affected the viability of their offspring in the seventeenth century. Changes in the marriage age of princesses may also have played a role. Between 1300 and 1500, almost half of the women of the houses of Hohenzollern and Nassau who married did so between the ages of twelve and fifteen. The same was true for about one-third of brides in the house of Wittelsbach during the same period. Among sixteenth-century dynasties throughout Europe, 54.1 percent of brides whose ages are known were less than twenty years old. In the seventeenth century, that percentage fell to 33.3 percent. Inasmuch as neonatal and perinatal death (the moments of highest infant mortality) peaks at both ends of the female fertility span, postponing marriage and pregnancy to a more favorable age inevitably affected the health of infant and mother positively.[14]

But more than anything, the survival of larger numbers of children—among them the males who are crucial to this study—was a function of the high reproductive rates among German princes in the sixteenth and seventeenth centuries. Increasing the pool of newborns raises the number of those likely to enjoy a normal life span. What accounts for the surge of princely offspring during this time? Customs peculiar to ruling and aristocratic houses probably had some influence. Breast-feeding, which temporarily suspends the menstrual cycle or at least lowers the chance of conception substantially, was widely practiced by the masses in early modern Europe but not by their urban and noble betters. Books recommending wet nursing were extremely rare in sixteenth-century Germany, but one that did, Oswald Gaebelkoven's *Artzneybuch* of 1595, was written by a man who practiced solely among the upper reaches of society. Within the first few months of birth, both the future Emperor Maximilian II and Duke Maximilian I of Bavaria (1573–1651) had wet nurses.[15]

Anthropologists have long noted however that reproductive patterns in any given class of society are not strictly a function of biological factors.[16] Confessional orientation and associated pressures can also play a major role. This striking elevation in birth and survival rates, generation upon generation, occurred during the Reformation era. We already have seen that sensitized Christian consciences guided many rulers' behavior toward their sons in their wills. It is therefore not improbable that those same religious feelings might have had some bearing on their manner of producing offspring as well.

Catholic and Protestant agreed upon the need to populate Creation as biblical imperative would have it, though the Roman preference for celibacy qualified this view somewhat. "Oh how blessed you are, how much more honorable and blessed is the fertility of this, your clerical designs compared to the profligacy of earthly marriage," exulted Aegidius Albertinus, the secretary of Maximilian I of Bavaria, in his *Hauspolizei* of 1602.[17] Such reservations did not trouble Luther. As he noted in "Vom ehelichen Leben," God's command to multiply was more than a simple order—it was a divine work implanted in nature. In his final years, the reformer urged others to follow the reproductive model of the ancient Israelites who he believed were highly fertile. Some of his most withering criticism was aimed at princes and noblemen who avoided having children, presumably for economic reasons. Luther called the practice "stupid" and a sign of original sin. The fruit of such ideas appeared in Cranach's woodcuts and drawings of 1538 and 1540. These show Christ blessing not a handful of children but swarms of them![18]

From the Protestant standpoint bountiful reproduction had a utilitarian side. The counts of Reuss von Plauen observed in a house compact of 1668 that God had established wedlock to insure not only the survival of humankind but of his church as well. Others were more openly altruistic. For Ernest the Pious, children were acts of God for which parents were only intermediaries.[19] Presumably the more heirs one had, the more opportunity one had to act as the Creator's agent.

Thus, a ruling house bent on continuity met no obstacle in Protestantism or Catholicism when it came to massive reproduction. Indeed, the reformed camp positively encouraged the practice. But high fertility would have been dynastically inconsequential had male off-spring been born out of wedlock. Young princes were politically significant only if their appearance took place in a formal matrimonial setting. Marriage conferred upon the children that it generated the cachet of legitimacy without which no house could defend its claim to be the exclusive source of rulers for very long. Any religious system that advocated marital fidelity was therefore fully at one with the imperatives of dynastic rule. Sixteenth- and seventeenth-century re-formers, both Protestant and Catholic, held precisely these positions. Furthermore, many princes took these exhortations very seriously.

All sides agreed that marriage was in some way a holy act. A divine plan dictated that husband and wife live together, said Duke William V of Bavaria in a marriage prayer. Trying to prevent the divorce of his sister Katherine and Sigismund August of Poland (1520–1572) who claimed that she had some loathsome disease, Emperor Maximilian II argued that "neither divine nor human law allowed a husband to repudiate his wife for such reasons." In his view the "bonds of mar-riage" were sacred. By neglecting his wife and seeking to separate himself from her altogether, Sigismund was incurring divine anger.[20] In the Protestant camp, one of Philip of Hesse's daughters deemed marriage a "holy duty." Maurice the Learned of Hesse-Kassel called his union with Agnes of Solms "a special dispensation of almighty God," a view in which the sons of Ernest the Pious concurred. Wives were no less convinced of this than their husbands. In 1567 Duchess Elisabeth of Saxony-Gotha begged Emperor Maximilian II to release her imprisoned husband, Duke John Frederick, "so that we can live as one together according to God's law."[21] Most eloquent of all was the guilt-ridden Philip of Hesse:

> Why has God himself created it [marriage] and never forbidden it? Why have God's angels served and aided it? Look at the book of Genesis and you will find it. Why have the patriarchs had wives, and so too the prophets? Why was Christ born? Is marriage so evil? Why did apostles such as Peter, Paul and others have wives? . . . It is certain that Christ himself was at a marriage and performed his first miracle there, the transformation of water into wine. The mother of Christ herself was the housewife and said, they have no wine.[22]

Princes of all Christian confessions in sixteenth- and seventeenth-century Germany took an exceedingly dim view of fornication, the most glaring violation of marital ties among their subjects. Convinced that illegitimate children angered God, Maximilian I of Bavaria issued several decrees throughout his long reign threatening fines, exile, and even death for adultery and illicit intercourse. Ernest the Pious allegedly cleared his lands of prostitutes altogether. Wolfgang of the Palatine-Zweibrücken believed that God condemned all sexual activity outside of wedlock and punished it mercilessly.[23]

Princes shared the same concerns for their families that they did for their subjects. If his younger sons could not find wives appropriate to their rank, Adolph Frederick of Mecklenburg-Schwerin (1588–1658) advised them in 1654 to conclude morganatic marriages. That way, or so reasoned the duke, the young men could avoid satisfying their passions illicitly.[24] At the beginning of the seventeenth century, the Calvinist Maurice of Hesse-Kassel married quickly after the death of his first wife, in part because of his desire to avoid sin.[25] So sophisticated and cosmopolitan a lady as Duchess Sophia of Braunschweig-Hannover, later to become an electress, was repelled by the easy sexual morals she saw on her only visit to Italy in 1664. "A German like myself," she said, "felt out of place in a country where one thinks of nothing but love, and where women believe themselves to be dishonored if they don't have admirers *{galans}*. I had always been taught that coquetery was wrong, and I found Italian morals contrary to that."[26] Seeking to persuade her bachelor brother, Landgrave William IV of Hesse-Kassel to marry, his sister Elisabeth reminded him that the Bible endorsed wedlock. Anyone who lived outside of it fell easily into "debauchery," as she primly termed it.[27] The prologue to the first version of Henry Julius of Braunschweig-Wolfenbüttel's play "Susanna" and the epilogue of the second stress the need for all classes of society to be exemplary in their sexual conduct. Midian, one of the two lechers who tempt Susanna into adultery, is a magistrate, reason enough for him to be blameless in his conduct, as the desperate heroine chides him.[28]

The best example of a German prince tormented by pangs of conscience over extramarital sexual relations was undoubtedly Landgrave Philip of Hesse. Often overlooked in the polemic surrounding his bigamous second marriage to Margaret von Saal is the main reason for the sensual prince's action—a final effort to save her soul and his. Even at the outset of his first union with Christina of Saxony in 1523, Philip had found her at best unsatisfactory and, at worst, repugnant. Unable to still his passionate nature, he began a long series of illicit liaisons.[29] At the same time, however, his religious scruples about his behavior mounted. In 1539 he refused to take communion, having learned from Paul that an adulterer or prostitute would be denied the heavenly kingdom. Self-discipline, however, was beyond him. Something close to compulsion drew him into fornication or "worse" with women.[30] In asking Luther's sanction of a second marriage, he vowed that pleasure was not his uppermost concern. Nor did it seem Christian and honorable to him to treat Margaret as a concubine, as Luther, Melanchthon, and Martin Bucer had advised him to do for a time.[31]

Thus both Protestant and Catholic princes of the Reformation, as much caught up as others in the religious sentiments of their age, attributed great moral importance to sexual relations and marriage. Heeding the call of conjugal fidelity left them with no alternative beyond their legal wives when they sought sexual fulfillment. Here, certainly, is our first clue to the high fertility rate among these men in the years between 1550 and 1675. Marriage, after all, can and often does, "have a strong tendency to increase fertility because it provides a guarantee of sexual access and of mutual support during the dual phases of a procreative career."[32] Modern demographic and social historians have often linked upsurges in illegitimacy with the loosening of the scruples that the Reformation and Counter-Reformation brought to Europe. Indeed, the slump in fecundity among Europe's ruling families between roughly 1650 and 1749 has been tied to looser moral standards among princes.[33] Logically and empirically, the obverse of this proposition should be true—namely, that stricter observance of such imperatives helps account for a striking upsurge in legitimate births.

But the heightened respect for marital fidelity was only one link between religious conviction and enhanced fecundity among German princes in the Reformation era. Spousal loyalty by itself will not enlarge the pool of heirs if intercourse between husband and wife is infrequent. Nature knows no better contraceptive than abstinence; had a prince foregone relations with mistresses, yet not sought his wife more frequently, the total issue of the union would not have increased so markedly.

The traditional Christian view of intercourse was positive only if the act took place within wedlock for procreative ends. Generally speaking, medieval theologians had downplayed marriage as a way of avoiding fornication, though this view had changed somewhat, especially since the fourteenth century. Such thinkers as Denis the Carthusian (1402–1481) and Martin le Maistre (1438–1481) affirmed the lawfulness of coitus between husband and wife on the grounds of mutual pleasure among other things. Le Maistre developed the notion of "conjugal chastity"—defined as "the mean between immodesty and insensibility"—that Christians of most persuasions eventually made a cornerstone of their ideas on spousal relationships. The Tridentine catechism did not explicitly condemn marriage as a check on fornication, and Peter Canisius, the spearhead of the Counter-Reformation in Central Europe, actually advocated it.[34] Sexual abstinence, however, remained the ideal from which all deviations were a sign of greater or lesser weakness.

The Protestant reformers, on the other hand, had special reasons to assign a high value to marital intercourse. Marriage was the instrument through which Luther struck back at the falsity of a priesthood that used the vow of celibacy as part of its claim to greater spirituality. While he continued to respect those who were truly chaste—believing that such men enjoyed a very special kind of grace—Luther taught that God had ordained marriage for most of mankind. Salvation, nevertheless, was not more difficult to reach because of that.[35]

In denying the specific holiness of celibacy, the Protestant reformers freed matrimony from the long-standing taint of spiritual imperfection. They also assigned a positive role in human affairs to sexual relations between man and wife—keeping both from illicit intercourse. Even though he admitted that marriage was not an imperative of the gospel, Luther viewed the institution as a part of God's law that served to check sin.[36]

In the eyes of Luther's followers and the Calvinists, who in some ways went even further, the legitimate union of husband and wife became a virtue, and chastity something of an abnormality. Although no one defended what was called "immoderate amorousness" and children ultimately sanctified both marriage and the marriage act, sexual relations between husband and wife for other than procreative purposes were not considered sinful in themselves.[37]

Probably no one will ever know the frequency of relations between German princes and their wives in the sixteenth and seventeenth centuries. But if occasional intercourse or outright chastity insures a low birthrate, increased numbers of births in ruling families certainly suggests more regular sexual concourse between princes and their wives. In one of royalty's more notable cases of spousal indifference in the seventeenth century—that of Louis XIII of France toward Anne of Austria, his Spanish wife—infrequent intercourse was clearly a factor in the infertility of the marriage. Quantitative evidence supports this conclusion as well. Unlike statistics for the general population, the age of the father seems to bear on the fertility of ruling families. There is a noticeable decline in their birthrates as the male gets older. Among European unions in which a prince married at the age of fifty or older, the percentage of couples without issue dropped from 50 percent in the period 1450–1549 to 30.8 percent during 1550–1649. That figure rebounded to 42.9 percent in the years 1650–1749, suggesting that princes in the previous hundred years had compensated for a decrease in biological vigor by more frequent intercourse with their wives.[38]

That the notoriously unfaithful among German princes often had few legitimate heirs further strengthens the hypothesis that their counterparts who sired large numbers of children took the teachings of Protestant and Catholic reformers on marriage and sexuality most earnestly indeed. Elector John George III of Saxony (1647–1691), a recognized philanderer, left only two legitimate children. The amatory feats of one of his sons, August II, found their way out of court gossip into story and song. Though he fathered literally hundreds of bastards, he had only one legitimate male heir. Some, of course, were productive both within and beyond the bonds of wedlock—Ernest August of Braunschweig-Hannover, for one.[39] But in the chancy world of genetics and premodern obstetrics, the safest avenue to dynastic continuity was frequent intercourse with one's legitimate wife. The open endorsement of such practices by religious reformers of the sixteenth and seventeenth centuries made them acceptable in ways not previously acknowledged. The unusually high birthrate among German ruling houses during this period was the likely result of these views.

Thus a religious reason was added to the already compelling dynastic interests that encouraged the siring of legitimate heirs. All these pressures were wholly supportive of the biological survival of any given house over time. But how did they affect the resources and potential power of that house if partible inheritance also played a key role in this system? Depending upon the number of sons they fathered, German rulers had to confront this problem as well. The issue knew no confessional boundaries. For Protestants, however, their faith held an embarrassing trap that would force them to make an agonizing choice between salvation and political self-interest.

For if it was a Christian couple's duty to have children, it was also their obligation to care for them. The stricture applied to rulers as well as the more common run of mankind. A particularly heavy opprobrium hung over those who tried to cheat juvenile princes out of their patrimonial due. Trying to settle a dispute over Maurice of Hesse-Kassel's will in the seventeenth century, Hesse-Kassel reminded Hesse-Darmstadt that both divine and natural law forbade the oppression of innocents and minors.[40] Such responsibilities did not stop with simple nurturing and basic education. Rather, they included launching one's offspring into the adult world with mate and property if at all possible. If one believed as did Elector John George of Saxony that marriage was something that "obedient daughters and virtuous princesses should engage in," then it was incumbent on him and those who thought as he did to find appropriate spouses for the young ladies in question. Luther himself believed that good fathers found suitable husbands and wives for their children.[41] Given the necessary relationship that lineage, property, and political status bore to one another, Germany's rulers probably took this task more to heart than did humbler folk.

Property divisions were a very natural way of meeting one's duties to one's offspring, especially the males among them. Indeed, the more one's family grew, the more some princes construed partible inheritance as a way of fulfilling their parental responsibilities. As the number of his offspring increased at the end of the sixteenth century, Henry of Braunschweig-Dannenberg (1533–1598) rued the agreement he had made with a nephew, Ernest of Braunschweig-Zelle, which awarded the latter the lion's share of their family lands.[42] It was the appearance of heirs that prompted Dukes John William and John Frederick of Saxony to arrange a division of their lands in 1566.[43] As long as they were the issue of Christian unions, sons of princes were deemed worthy of inheritances, regardless of the order of birth. Though he abdicated in 1627, Maurice the Learned of Hesse-Kassel took care of the children of his second marriage in a codicil to his testament of 1632. Monies acquired after his resignation and not needed to pay off debts were to be used exclusively to establish inheritances for these offspring. Landgrave William V (1602–1637), Maurice's oldest son, regretted his father's generosity. He conceded, however, that all princes of Christian marriages merited consideration in their sires' testaments.[44]

Thus, Christian conscience and testamentary tradition spoke in one voice regarding the general duty of Germany's princes to care for their children. But the two imperatives were not so compatible when the means to provide for all this were at issue. This was especially true for the Protestants. For one thing, the religious significance of marriage imparted an otherworldly air to the institution that did not stop with childbearing and rearing but touched the mating process as well. With higher values in mind, many German princes downplayed material considerations such as marrying in order to better one's territorial position. No prince, regardless of his convictions, would turn down a splendid dowry if it came his way.[45] However, such windfalls were neither to be expected nor sought after.

Devout Protestants, of course, did not marry Catholics, especially in the sixteenth century. And, to be sure, by shunning brilliant marriages, German princes in the sixteenth and seventeenth centuries may have been putting a spiritual gloss upon inescapable practical limitations. Even if they had chosen to go abroad for mates, as the Habsburgs and Wittelsbachs did, most German princes did not have the wherewithal to underwrite the nuptial contracts routine among their counterparts in Spain, Italy, and France. The matrimonial choices of Germany's rulers were therefore confined to native princesses, who once they became wives were routinely cut out of their patrimonies and instead received money settlements at marriage.[46]

But even when one takes all these factors into account, the princes still seem to have gone out of their way to downplay financial interests when choosing wives. Just as they condemned primogeniture because it reflected undue concern with secular affairs, so too great and foreign marriages were heavily criticized. John William of Saxony-Weimar urged his sons not to marry abroad, thereby condemning them to lives of comparative penury, but no matter. *"Uxor prudens a Domino datur,"* he assured them. Whatever good a princess brought to the lands of her husband was through "Christian marriage," something with which the overly ambitious among humankind had presumably very little to do.[47]

For all that he wanted to enlarge the financial resources of Hesse-Kassel, Landgrave William IV enjoined his son, Maurice, not to aim for a great marriage but for one with an honorable and pious lady.[48] And for resolute modesty, it was hard to surpass the counts of Reuss. Marriage, as they saw it, should be contracted with houses that were neither above nor beneath them. That way, the selection of a bride would show the individual prince's wish for "true piety, sound reason [and] countly and lordly qualities, morals, and virtues" rather than for a large income and external splendor.[49]

The major German Catholic houses, on the other hand, labored under no such scruples. Though the marital morals of the Habsburgs and Wittelsbachs in the sixteenth and seventeenth centuries were perhaps even more straitlaced than those of their Protestant counterparts, their faith apparently set no serious limitations on ambition where dynastic interests were concerned. The Austrian Habsburgs who followed Ferdinand I were not comfortable with Spanish ways (indeed, often despised them), yet they never doubted that part of their power base was the continued marital connection with their cousins from Madrid. The Wittelsbachs cultivated the Habsburgs as well as princesses from Lorraine and Savoy for the same reason and with no pangs of conscience. Indeed, Emperor Maximilian II recommended a younger duchess of Lorraine rather than her elder sister to Albert V of Bavaria for his son William V on the grounds that the lady in question was not only better looking but promised a richer dowry as well.[50]

Why were Catholic marriage strategies so much more flexible than Protestant ones? The Catholic faith and its position in the empire of the Reformation and Counter-Reformation clearly played a major role. Unlike the Lutherans, the pool of eligible co-religionists was very small, leaving those loyal to the Church of Rome with no choice but to search for husbands and wives abroad, even though the choices there were sometimes distressingly narrow. For this reason, Duke, later Elector, Maximilian I of Bavaria was willing to consider a Florentine bride for his brother, Duke Albert VI (1584–1666). Maximilian, William V (Maximilian's father), Albert V, and those who advised them were anxious to conserve their revenues for the defense of Catholicism. Nothing, obviously, was more contrary to this goal than supporting younger sons whose wives had no greater or even lesser incomes than a prince's own. Albert V specified that a younger son, Duke Ferdinand (1550–1608), seek permission from his father or eldest brother to marry. Failure to do so would be cause to revoke his allowance. The lone exception to this rule was if Ferdinand arranged a marriage for himself with a very well-endowed princess.[51]

Catholic houses were also more experimental in their approach to inheritance practices as well, and in the case of the major dynasties, for the same reason. Both the Habsburgs and the Wittelsbachs were keenly aware that the survival of their beleaguered faith in central Europe hung in large part on the way they handled their dynastic resources. During the reign of Ferdinand I, who controlled all the Habsburg territories, financial contributions for the "Austrian Circle," one of the ten regional groupings established for military purposes in the empire in 1512, were drawn from the "Upper Austrian" treasury in Innsbruck. When Ferdinand's second son, Archduke Ferdinand II, received the Tyrol as his patrimonial share, he found that he was still called upon to make these payments, even though his total resources were far smaller than his father's. His younger brother, Archduke Charles, who took over "Inner Austria" with its capital in Graz, refused to make any contributions because, in his view, he had to shoulder the greatest responsibility for defense against the Turks.[52] As early as 1578, Ferdinand's grandsons grudgingly agreed with their councillors that any formal division of the Austrian lands would create dwarf territories that singly could not support any of them adequately. Such ill-considered measures would only play into the hands of their mortal enemies, the Turks.[53]

Similar considerations led those same grandsons to move toward the abolition of partible inheritance. Childless to a man, gout-ridden, and generally enfeebled, they debated the issue extensively between 1615 and 1618. Each of them was theoretically eligible to offer himself as a candidate for German king and emperor and, as direct descendants of the eldest male in the line of Ferdinand I, to claim the right to part of the Habsburg patrimony. Indeed, the imperial position had passed from brother to brother several times in the past fifty years or so. Ferdinand I had followed his sibling Charles V, and Matthias I had succeeded his elder brother, Rudolph II. Matthias had actually made his brother Archduke Albert (1559–1621) his heir in the Austrian lands themselves.

The strong possibility that their Spanish cousins might put forth a claim to both the imperial title as well as the Habsburg central European lands weighed heavily on their minds. But they also asked what would be the best step for the house of Habsburg given its crucial place in the cause of Catholic Christendom. The situation called for self-sacrifice, and the Habsburg brothers had a strong enough sense of their mission to yield. Rather than press their rights, they called upon their young nephew at the court of Styria, the future Emperor Ferdinand II, to serve as head of their house. His genetic vigor had already been proven in his siring of sons, one of whom would be Emperor Ferdinand III (1608–1657).[54]

This same concern—that family and territorial resources had to be concentrated in order to defend Catholicism—was argued even more eloquently in Munich in 1610. At issue was whether Maximilian I should increase the allowance of his brother Archduke Albert. An appeal had been made along traditional lines to the ruling duke's brotherly affection and conscience. Worried over already heavy taxation, a restless peasantry, and scarcity of private ducal means, Maximilian's advisers were loath to grant the request: "Since your princely grace wishes to do far more than what [your father's] testament requires and show feeling, the result will be that, when the need arises, your princely grace . . . will be able to give far less support to the religion and to the fatherland." Experience had shown that "all the Protestant electors and estates look to your princely grace, as do the Catholic estates, for whom you are a refuge[;] it is this very respect that the Protestant estates have for your princely highness, that has been of great value to the Catholic religion, which will diminish, since its resources will gradually be exhausted (as cannot be otherwise if this request is granted)."[55]

Maximilian's fraternal duties toward Albert had already been fulfilled with the presentation of an appanage in the county of Haag. If the sole result of such generosity was to prompt more such requests, then any "rational person" (*"yeder verstendiger"*) should reevaluate the policy. That only "private convenience" (*"Privat Commoditet"*), rather than the general welfare, was considered in such affairs was altogether lamentable.[56] Such language recommended not only a specific decision but a general policy as well. Where the preservation of the faith and, by extension, anything else of public significance was concerned, personal and family feeling had little place in a prince's calculations.

Maximilian certainly espoused these views, though they were not original to him. Rather they were part of a larger set of ideas that had found a home at the Bavarian court in the last decade of the sixteenth century. The most likely source of them was the neo-Stoic political thinker Justus Lipsius (1547–1606). Born in the Netherlands, Lipsius was increasingly in vogue among Catholic princes in the late sixteenth century following his conversion to their faith in 1591. The following year, Maximilian's father, William V, had tried to coax him to Bavaria. Though the philosopher did not go, his ideas took root among Wittelsbach advisers.

Central to Lipsius's system was the primacy of natural law and the imperative to strengthen the state according to these principles. The conduct of public affairs allowed no room for sentiment or tradition. Political responsibility was a test of self-discipline for both a ruler and his subjects.[57]

Such views were obviously congenial to the consolidation of princely power through the introduction of primogeniture. How, though, did the favoring of one member of the house, although necessary for political and confessional purposes, square with the Christian paternal obligation to provide equally for one's offspring? The answer is that it did not. There was a way to substitute equity for equality with appanages. In this procedure cadet princes were given allowances and territorial livings but no effective role in government. By the beginning of the seventeenth century, a number of princely houses were engaging in this practice—most notably the Wittelsbachs and Habsburgs—though some Protestant dynasties were trying it as well. A young prince did not fare badly by such arrangements. When a father, through his testament, decided to introduce the rule of the firstborn, an imperial commission usually came into being to see that appanaged sons were treated fairly. The same considerations were applied to allowances. In Bavaria, for example, councillors argued that since the *Deputat* of Albert VI, supposedly fifty-five thousand florins annually, surpassed that of imperial Habsburg archdukes, the younger Wittelsbach had little cause for complaint.[58]

Furthermore, in the sixteenth and seventeenth centuries it was very difficult to distinguish many appanages from partible inheritances since they had something of the same impact. Allowances of younger princes came from the income of the father or firstborn male sibling. These revenues were very uncertain, linked as they were to the yields of a prince's domains and the willingness of estates to make contributions. Settlement of some land and peoples on younger sons was still therefore common. Some of these arrangements conferred a substantial amount of territorial sovereignty as well, especially in the seventeenth century. It was not until these considerations were fully converted into money payments, a development of the nineteenth century, that the economic consequences of primogeniture could be fully enjoyed.[59]

The Bavarian princes, at least, did not see the appanage system as a complete break with primogeniture, but rather as something of a compromise with the practice needed to perpetuate it.[60] And, in one way, the arrangement left a *primogenitus,* especially one not well endowed with male offspring, with some important advantages. In 1602 Duke Ferdinand of Bavaria received the county of Wartenberg and its title with the clear understanding that he had no further claim to anything in the Wittelsbach patrimony. If the line of the male *primogenitus*—in this case his nephew, Maximilian—were to die out, however, Ferdinand's sons and their descendants would have the right of succession in Munich assured to them.[61] Thus the nagging problem of dynastic continuity could be addressed without undue burdens on the resources of the entire house.

But appanages, however they met the formalities of parental obligation, had less to recommend them in the eyes of most younger sons. Even as they received allowances, younger brothers were relegated to the status of supplicants, dependent upon the good will of their father or eldest brother and relieved of their right to codirection of their dynasty's affairs. Maximilian I of Bavaria agreed to insure the marriage provision (*Heiratsgut*) of his brother Albert so long as it was understood that he was acting spontaneously, not out of some obligation. The central ducal treasury in Munich, even under the spendthrift William V, kept a close accounting of expenditures from appanages and held a very low opinion of profligate cadets. As a memorandum of 1610 to Maximilian I indicated, there was little point in conducting a fiscally responsible government if some of its profits were handed over to someone who squandered them. Estates, too, denied requests for the improvement of allowances. Nor did the holder of a Bavarian appanage necessarily have its resources to himself. William V and his brother Ferdinand agreed in 1580 that both had rights to wood in the latter's appanage of Hohenschwangau. By the end of his career, Maximilian toyed with the idea of making his younger male relatives governors and military men, in effect turning them into service personnel rather than political equals who deserved special financial considerations because of their family relationship.[62]

But Catholics had a better way to enjoy the advantages of primogeniture, yet live with their consciences over the treatment of younger sons. They could still arrange appropriate livings for their offspring in the church. In such a fashion could fathers and brothers behave in a just and Christian way without seriously diluting the resources of their houses. The sons of Maximilian II did not feel in any way constrained to include their brother Archduke Albert in discussions of territorial divisions in 1577 and 1578 because he was already a cardinal.[63]

The higher echelons of society throughout Europe, Germany included, had long dealt with the problem of surplus children, both legitimate and illegitimate, by finding them appropriate clerical livings. At one time or another, almost all houses resorted to the practice to keep from splintering their properties too badly. It was for this reason that the counts of Hanau agreed in 1458 that all but one legitimate son would remain celibate in any given generation. With the beginning of the fifteenth century, the Palatine Wittelsbachs regularly sent second sons into the church to avoid fragmentation of their widely scattered domains. In 1465 Count Henry of Württemberg turned to an ecclesiastical career for the same reason.

Catholic princes did not always take kindly to clerical roles. The youngest son of Albert IV of Bavaria, Duke Ernest (1500–1560), felt no spiritual calling and complained that he could aspire to no more than the title of count with an income of 4,000 gulden a year from his elder brother.[64] A nephew, also Ernest by name (1554–1612) and the bishop of Freising at age eleven, doubted that he had the character for the office.[65] Though comfortably ensconced as bishop of both Passau and Strassburg, Archduke Leopold, the younger brother of Emperor Ferdinand II, continued, as we have already seen, to chafe at his fate. He eventually renounced his vows and persuaded his brother to let him found a separate, though short-lived, Habsburg line in the Tyrol.[66]

But whatever reservations a young Habsburg or Wittelsbach harbored about ecclesiastical callings, he could not seriously accuse his father of treating him inequitably. Such sons often continued to draw allowances from their fathers or eldest brothers. The prince-bishop, for this is what he often became, was assured that as a high church functionary he could maintain a lifestyle befitting his dynastic station. The entrance in 1607 of Archduke Leopold to his new see in Strassburg was as carefully orchestrated as a royal procession itself. A retinue of 334 persons, including two princes and eighty-six noblemen, accompanied him, along with 316 horses.[67] The sixteenth-century Ernest of Bavaria used his sees in Passau and Salzburg for commercial investment schemes that were both imaginative and lucrative. Careful never to take final vows, Ernest withdrew from Salzburg with his profits in 1554 to a fief received from the Habsburgs in Glatz. Here he maintained a comfortable bachelor existence, easily able to support the six illegitimate children whom he fathered.[68]

If, by chance, the incomes from church livings did not reach expected levels, a princely cleric could still count on his father for help. Following heavy damage by the Spanish to the Rhineland holdings of the archbishopric of Cologne, Duke William V of Bavaria pressed to have Madrid compensate these losses. His son, Ferdinand, was coadjutor in the Rhenish see, possessed of "many titles and little income" ("*vhil titl und wenig einkhomen*"), thereby giving him a claim to William's scarce funds for support.[69]

Ecclesiastical careers locked no one out of active participation in secular dynastic affairs. Indeed, clerical appointments conferred political roles that younger sons who remained out of the church would not enjoy. The bishopric of Freising was not particularly rich when the eleven-year-old Ernest of Bavaria acquired it in 1566. Nevertheless, it conferred upon him the status of imperial prince with the right to vote in the diet.[70] When receiving the regalia of their lands from the emperor, the heads of German princely dynasties often insisted that these be given in the names of all their brothers, lay and clerical. The margrave of Brandenburg, for example, asked this of Charles V at the Diet of Worms in 1521 for his notorious younger sibling, Albert, the bishop of Mainz. A young prince who had become a cathedral canon had little trouble returning to secular life, if the affairs of his house demanded it, so long as he was not a subdeacon. Only with that office did one begin to need a papal dispensation in order to break the vow of celibacy. But such concessions were often forthcoming when the survival of a ruling family was at stake. Though bishop of both

Passau and Strassburg, Archduke Leopold had taken only lower vows. Renouncing both sees in 1625, he was absolved from these bonds and married in the same year.[71]

But even if they chose to remain bishops, as most of them did, the clerical Habsburgs and Wittelsbachs were playing crucial roles in the affairs of their houses and of their confessions during the sixteenth and seventeenth centuries. One way of stemming the spread of Protestantism was to put members of these committed Catholic dynasties into important ecclesiastical positions. Albert V of Bavaria was especially sensitive to this matter. Indeed, where more clerical vacancies existed than sons, both he and the Habsburgs revived plural benefices. Though curbed by the church at the Council of Trent, the practice was acceptable in Rome when Catholic sway over the bishoprics in northern Germany was threatened. Proceeding jauntily under the motto *"omnia,"* Albert's son Ernest controlled the sees of Freising, Hildesheim, Liège, Cologne, and Münster. A contemporary, Archduke Sigismund Francis of Austria (1630–1665), was bishop of Augsburg, Gurk, and Trent; Sigismund Francis's uncle, Leopold William (1614–1662), had two archbishoprics and five bishoprics to his credit.[72]

Both princes and those who advised them time and again vowed that the honor and reputation of their families were at stake in ecclesiastical elections and that their outcome was the concern of their entire house.[73] As a candidate for the archbishopric of Strassburg in 1607, Archduke Leopold took the matter to heart not only because of himself but for the sake of all the "esteemed" house of Austria.[74] By becoming a clergyman, the late sixteenth-century Ernest of Bavaria grudgingly acknowledged that moral improvements on his part would at least benefit the Wittelsbach dynasty as a whole.[75] The attitude endured well into the eighteenth century. In 1779 Empress Maria Theresa's (1717–1780) foreign minister, Prince Kaunitz, pointed out to her all the virtues of having her son, Archduke Maximilian (1756–1801), as archbishop of Cologne. Not only would he have a better living than the mastership of the Teutonic Order would bring him, but the archbishopric would bring great honor to the entire house. It would also have enormous strategic and political benefits. The Habsburgs would have more influence in the electoral college of the empire, and the location of the episcopate on the Rhine would allow its occupant to close that waterway if necessary. It would also be a nuisance to the king of Prussia who had Westphalian holdings.[76]

Nor did accepting a clerical or paraclerical life consign one to an essentially passive role in the internal affairs of one's house. Archduke Maximilian (1558–1618), a younger brother of Emperor Rudolph II, was a case in point. Master of the Teutonic Order in Vienna and therefore celibate, he was nevertheless the driving force behind the Habsburg succession arrangements at the beginning of the seventeenth century through which Ferdinand of Styria eventually became head of that house.[77]

Thus the Catholic Habsburgs and Wittelsbachs were not limited to their patrimonies in meeting obligations to their sons and brothers equitably. Clerical positions and incomes as well as the continued opportunity to play central roles in their dynasty's confessional concerns allowed—in fact, encouraged—princes to retain their status even as they renounced the hope of legitimate heirs. Indeed, that hope was not altogether removed, given the ease with which princes could withdraw from many ecclesiastical positions.

The availability of such livings certainly made it far easier for Catholic dynasties to introduce primogeniture, reap the advantages it conferred, and still be at peace with their consciences. Even their clergy supported it. Three bishops were among those who recommended at the end of the sixteenth century that the Styrian branch of the Austrian Habsburgs adopt rule of the firstborn.[78] And it seems likely that feelings of guilt and worries over fraternal disaffection could be eased by endowing disinherited younger sons or brothers with rich benefices. Only with the introduction of primogeniture did the Habsburgs and Wittelsbachs consistently send legitimate sons from each generation into the church. Both dynasties, it should be noted, had been among the most active in territorial partitions throughout the Middle Ages. Once primogeniture was fixed in the Austrian lands, no generation was without a male clergyman until the reign of Leopold I—despite the absence of large numbers of male progeny. The same pattern was followed by the Wittelsbachs. As soon as Albert IV introduced the custom in Bavaria, he had his second son, Ludwig, tonsured and arranged for him to become provost of Freising.[79]

Could this greater interest in placing sons in ecclesiastical positions on the part of the Habsburgs and the Wittelsbachs have been caused by an upsurge in piety during the Catholic reform rather than by a change in inheritance practices? Was it simply a matter of religious geopolitics? Evidence does not support these arguments, either singly or together. Albert IV determined that Ludwig should enter the clergy before the Reformation was even a fact. Few Catholic rulers were as devout as Emperor Ferdinand I or as bent on strengthening their faith through the appointment of trustworthy clergy. Yet, Ferdinand followed traditional practice when he divided his patrimony among his three sons. Once the Habsburgs decided to observe primogeniture, the equally pious Emperors Ferdinand II and Ferdinand III sent sons into the church, even as their line thinned out dangerously through the seventeenth century.

The role of ecclesiastical positions in discouraging partible inheritance among Catholics becomes even clearer when we examine the inheritance practices of some of Germany's lesser Catholic dynasties such as the Fürstenbergs, Schönborns, Oettingens, and Fuggers, the last raised to countly status by Ferdinand I in the sixteenth century. The Fürstenbergs divided into two lines around the middle of the century. Throughout the seventeenth century, the main branch included among its members two prince-bishops of Strassburg, one abbot of Murbach and Luders, and other ecclesiastical figures. A couple of sons found employ in the French army, and one became a *Statthalter* for the elector of Saxony. No further divisions of territory took place in this line. In the new line of Fürstenberg-Mösskirch, however, an additional division did take place. Following this split, the older Fürstenberg-Mösskirch line began to send sons into the church and ceased to split its holdings.

The counts of Oettingen created three lines for themselves, one of which was Protestant. The Catholics numbered exactly one clerical official among them and continued to divide. The Protestant counts of Oettingen-Oettingen interestingly enough did not seem to practice partible inheritance. This, however, was probably because they produced many more daughters than sons, and among the latter, bachelorhood and premature death were the rule. The counts of Schönborn had numerous sons throughout the seventeenth century, yet avoided dividing their territories by finding clerical positions for themselves throughout the empire. The seven male heirs of Count Melchior Frederick (1644–1717) illustrate the point neatly. Five won major ecclesiastical offices. Francis George became archbishop of Trier and bishop of Worms; Damian Hugo became bishop of Speyer and Constance and a cardinal as well; Frederick Carl was bishop of Bamberg and Würzburg, where John Philip Francis too eventually became bishop. The Fuggers, by way of contrast, numbered no churchmen among them and continued to divide. There were, obviously, just so many offices available, and not all families had access to them. Even the Habsburgs and the Wittelsbachs came into conflict over the distribution of such turf.[80] The same pattern was to be found in Catholic appanages. Maximilian I's brother, Albert VI, married Mechthild of Leuchtenberg and later exchanged these acquired lands with his older brother for other territories. No division took place at any point in these maneuvers, however, since both of Albert's sons became clergy. Religion, politics, and dynastic self-interest thus posed no inherent contradiction for Catholics. The comparative unity of the Habsburg and Wittelsbach territories by the middle of the seventeenth century bespoke that relationship.

Lutherans and Calvinists were not so fortunate. The secularization of church lands had not deprived them completely of clerical resting places for surplus sons. The Ecclesiastical Reservation accompanying the Peace of Augsburg in 1555 forbade Roman prelates who became Protestants to take their territorial incomes and holdings with them. It did not prohibit cathedral canons from electing Lutherans as bishops. As Protestantism spread throughout Germany in the sixteenth century, confessors of the Augustana appeared in many cathedral chapters. Lübeck, Osnabrück, Halberstadt, and several other sees had both Protestant and Catholic canons. As witnesses to what, in their opinion, was the pure gospel, Lutherans argued that incomes from church properties should fall to them rather than to those who spoke for the anti-Christ in Rome. Even though they did not receive the required papal confirmation, Protestants regularly administered the lands of these episcopates until the Peace of Westphalia finally regulated their status.[81]

At the height of the first enthusiasms accompanying the Lutheran reform, Philip of Hesse had scornfully chided parents who were far more interested in securing rich benefices for their children than in fulfilling God's wishes.[82] As they faced the problem of providing for their numerous progeny or siblings, later Protestant princes were not so sure. Contemplating the tenacity with which younger sons held to partible inheritance in the latter half of the sixteenth century, William IV of Hesse, Philip's oldest son, looked back on pre-Reformation traffic in clerical offices with genuine nostalgia.[83] Those Protestant princes who did have some control over who administered the church lands that remained in their territories found it far easier to live with primogeniture. In reaffirming the custom in his branch of the house in 1582, Duke Julius of Braunschweig-Lüneburg (1528–1589) urged his firstborn son not to turn his siblings away empty-handed. Rather they should be installed in the ecclesiastical foundations of Minden and Halberstadt, than under the supervision of their house. In this way, the young men could enjoy "rich princely incomes."[84] Having gone through a painful territorial division with one brother, Duke John Albert of Mecklenburg-Schwerin (1525–1576) ordered the introduction of primogeniture in his line in his testament of 1573. To still the objections of another brother, Duke Christopher (1537–1592), and to prevent further splits of his lands, he promised the latter that he would be made coadjutor of Riga, where he would find a suitable income. John Albert also held out the hope that Christopher would be named prince bishop of Ratzeburg.[85]

But there were even fewer of these positions for Protestants than there were for Catholics. Furthermore, when many of these lands were completely secularized after 1648 and fully incorporated into dynastic holdings, Protestant princes seeking to treat their sons justly, yet to preserve some semblance of territorial integrity, were once again adversely affected. The house of Hannover suffered especially.[86]

Thus, for Germany's Protestant rulers, religion and biology had proven benevolent agents in meeting one imperative of the dynastic system—production of heirs in large numbers. They were altogether incompatible with another imperative of that system—providing the resources to support these heirs. Catholics had a much easier time in reconciling the oneness of their houses, fulfilling their parental obligations to their children, and retaining a form of territorial integrity. For them, religion and reason of state were not so far apart. The gulf for the Protestants, however, had by the seventeenth century grown very wide indeed.

CHAPTER III
CHANGING VALUES, CHANGING TIMES

Religious scruples had kept the princes of early modern Germany true to their historical preference for equal inheritances. Religious conviction dovetailed neatly with the political requirement that they have an abundance of legitimate male heirs. Religious precept lent solid support to the proper marital arrangements for fathering such offspring. So seamless a structure of values and practical needs actively discouraged the adoption of primogeniture. The Catholic prince who found good livings for his cadets in the church was, however, in a somewhat better position to abolish partible inheritance with a clear conscience. Not having adequate access to such offices, his Protestant counterpart had no other way to meet his obligations to his heirs than to split the resources of his house. From all this one can only conclude that Protestantism was less helpful to the consolidation of princely power in Germany than the conventional wisdom would have it. Allegiance to long-standing inheritance practices, reinforced by their faith, had ensnared many Lutheran and Calvinist rulers in a vicious circle that circumscribed their potential influence and that of the lands and peoples they governed.

Examples appear wherever one looks for them in the empire of the sixteenth and seventeenth centuries. Nothing commonly recognized as interest of state was well served by the system. Houses were ever at odds among themselves over local, imperial, or foreign issues. Sometimes these differences were relatively trivial, involving no more than cousins soliciting votes on behalf of rival candidates for the emperorship or thwarting one another's marriage schemes.[1] Sometimes they were truly destructive. While quarreling among themselves over ancient land claims, all branches of a house sometimes came away as losers. Duke Ernest August of Braunschweig-Hannover walked off with Saxony-Lauenburg in the seventeenth century while both ducal and electoral Wettins quarreled over its title.[2]

Braunschweig-Lüneburg and Braunschweig-Wolfenbüttel were on opposite sides during the Thirty Years' War because of a local conflict between them over the bishopric of Hildesheim. Lüneburg fought in the Habsburg-imperial camp, Wolfenbüttel with the Protestants. Neither profited from their positions. Large chunks of the Wolfenbüttel inheritance were given to imperial generals as fiefs after the battle of Lutter in 1626, as was to be expected. But Duke George, the Habsburg supporter, fared no better. While he was rewarded with Grübenhagen, his plans to enlarge his territories by adding church lands to them came to nought. A son of the emperor was named to the see of Halberstadt, and Prince Ferdinand of Bavaria (1577–1650) became bishop of Hildesheim, the original bone of contention between the Braunschweig lines. The entire war and the destructive toll it took was precipitated in part by intradynastic rivalry. This conflict stemmed from the jealousy that the Munich Wittelsbachs had long harbored toward their relatives in the Palatinate for their control of the one electoral dignity in the house and the precedence associated with it in the imperial diet.[3]

Territorial particularism fostered confessional particularism and the other way around, thereby making conflicts meaner and more intractable still. When Landgrave Maurice of Hesse-Kassel, the grandson of the arch-Lutheran Philip, embraced Calvinism, vexed relations in that house were further envenomed. His relatives in Darmstadt labeled the move a "deformation," setting the tone for future discourse between the sides. That his eldest son was a Lutheran and his second son a Calvinist made a territorial division of Elector Frederick III of the Palatinate all the more hotly disputed.[4]

Theological differences between the universities of Jena, in ducal Saxony-Weimar, and Wittenberg, in the electorate, made the battle for control of the former institution even stormier between the two lines. Under the patronage of Elector August, Wittenberg grew into a center for moderate Lutherans, the Philippists, who were followers of Melanchthon. Jena, on the other hand, was controlled by more rigorous adherents of the new faith, the supporters of Flacius Illyricus. In 1572, as a difficult and complicated territorial dispute within the Saxon dynasty peaked, the professors at the universities were quarreling over the meaning of the Lord's Supper. The Philippists took a more symbolic and mystical approach to the question of the real presence in the Sacrament; the dogmatists of Jena viewed it far more literally. Elector August accused the Flacians of fomenting religious troubles in his own lands, especially in his schools and churches. When Duke John William of Saxony-Weimar died, August charged that the former's Flacian advisers had encouraged their ruler to draw up a will making them, rather than August, guardians for the duke's minor sons.[5] Religious differences made it easier for the several branches of one dynasty to wage outright war against one another. In 1539, a Habsburg ally, the Catholic Henry of Braunschweig-Wolfenbüttel, tried with his brother, Archbishop Christopher of Bremen (1487–1558), to seize the lands of his enthusiastically Lutheran cousin, Ernest of Braunschweig-Lüneburg (1497–1546).[6]

Long before the Reformation it was clear that such territorial divisions could weaken potentially powerful dynasties for centuries to come. The house compact of 1329 between Emperor Ludwig the Bavarian (1282–1347) and his nephews gave the latter the Palatinate and Upper Palatinate. The agreement opened the way to excluding

Ludwig's line from the Imperial College of Electors. The Rhenish Wittelsbachs subsequently sold Emperor Charles IV a generous portion of the Upper Palatinate; when their Luxembourg sovereign set the numbers of electors at seven in the Golden Bull of 1356, it was they, not their Bavarian cousins, who received one of those offices in perpetuity.[7] Philip of Hesse's territorial division among his nine sons in the sixteenth century laid to rest any prospects that his house had to expand into the Rhineland and Westphalia. The leading role of the principality within the concert of German princes also came to an end.[8] Partible inheritance hobbled many princes economically as well as politically. The dwarf principalities fashioned by some of the divisions were all but useless financially. By the time the line of the Limpurg counts died out in the eighteenth century, one of them had enjoyed rights to 5/96 of the town of Gaildorf, which numbered only fourteen hundred inhabitants. Another count could claim only 1/96 of the settlement's revenues, so often had these been partitioned.

Ludwig the Bavarian's territorial division with his Rhenish cousins in the fourteenth century gave the latter control over the iron fields of the Ruhr. The Bavarian Wittelsbachs were thereby forever cut off from that important resource. As the size of individual territories shrank, princes became increasingly dependent upon their territorial nobles, prelates, and cities for funds. In 1392 a committee of the various Bavarian estates supervised a partition that created Bavaria-Munich, Bavaria-Ingolstadt, and Bavaria-Landshut. With such power in their hands, these bodies were able to ward off ducal absolutism until well into the sixteenth century.[9]

Partible inheritance penalized both the ambitious prince as well as one who wished only to cultivate a lifestyle in keeping with his station.[10] Not only were major resources and encumbrances such as incomes and debts divided, but, as was the case among the Thuringian counts of Schwarzburg in 1574, supplies of wood and wine as well. The sons of Philip of Hesse's first marriage split their father's artillery and munitions along with his clothes, jewelry, silver place settings, horses, and harnesses. The most capable of the brothers, Landgrave William IV of Hesse-Kassel, was especially ill served by the agreement. Only the equipment he personally had won while campaigning with Elector Maurice of Saxony in the 1550s remained in his hands.[11]

Productive accumulation of dynastic resources, not to mention rational management of them, was often compromised and sometimes not considered at all. From Hesse-Kassel's tax revenues of approximately 130,384 florins in 1566, Landgrave William IV received 65,959. This was the lion's share, to be sure, but in the name of fraternal equality, the rest went to his brothers and stepbrothers the following year. After his death in 1564, Emperor Ferdinand I left his three sons a potential income of 872,394 florins, which the brothers decided to divide equally. Since the new emperor, Maximilian II, had received lower Austria, financially the weakest part of the Habsburg patrimony, his siblings had to compensate him from their domains if equality was to persist among them. Ferdinand of the Tyrol (1529–1595) therefore turned over 76,206 florins to his older brother, while Archduke Charles of Styria gave up 6,386 florins. One of the most economically bizarre of all German territorial partitions took place in 1566 when ducal Saxony was divided for six years with one center in Weimar and the other in Coburg. At the end of the first three years, John William in Coburg was to change places with John Frederick in Weimar. Each year, however, both were to report the earnings from their respective territories to one another. Whoever had more would give enough to the poorer brother to equalize the two incomes. John William himself called the arrangement "unusual."[12]

Territorial partitions encouraged separate courts with separate bureaucracies, in itself a burden on dynastic revenues. Some princes met the challenge of limited resources by becoming careful managers—William IV of Hesse-Kassel is an archexample. Others gave little or no thought to the morrow and became problems to both themselves and their houses. Despite all of William IV's admonitions, his younger brother, Philip, by the time of his death in 1583, owed creditors 145,345 florins from his holdings in Rheinfels-Katzenelnbogen. Debt service on that sum alone cost 6,500 annually, 132 florins more than the entire income of the territory.[13] Nor did individual enterprise and initiative thrive where brothers continued to hold some resources in common. The division of Saxony-Weimar in 1640 stipulated that gold, silver, and copper mines were to stay under collective control. Should any of the three princes involved wish to improve those facilities within the lands allotted to him, he had to serve written notification of his intentions. If his brothers did not respond within three months, he could proceed. If they refused his request, he could do nothing. [14]

Even if a prince did come to rule his house's lands alone, he could not always disavow territorial obligations to his brothers or keep them from making claims on new acquisitions. Such was the fate of Landgrave William V of Hesse-Kassel, who through an agreement in 1627 became the *alleinregierender Herr*. Although he had sole responsibility for the government of the principality and its costs, he had to deliver certain lands debt-free as compensation to his siblings. Future acquisitions through purchase or conquest in his branch of the house were to be divided in quarters among his brothers; new fiefs were to be vested collectively in all of them. [15]

Countless man-hours flew by in arranging these divisions, and still more in coping with their consequences. Many princes spent far more time on such matters than they did on military, diplomatic, or political affairs. Emperor Maximilian II and his brother Ferdinand bickered interminably with one another over shares each owed to dowries for their married sisters or for maintenance of those who had cloistered themselves. [16] The time of councillors was eaten up as well. During 1627–1628 five months of meetings among representatives of both sides were needed to reconcile the claims of Landgraves William V of Hesse-Kassel and George of Hesse-Darmstadt. Eight years went by before a settlement was reached in a four-way division of the Counts of Schwarzburg's holdings. [17] Talents of all sorts were called upon, especially when disagreements arose. A watercolorist provided visual aids in a quarrel between the dukes of Saxony in 1571. By drawing an outline map of each man's lands, then adding little *F*'s and *W*'s to indicate castles and administrative districts, he identified the holdings of Dukes John Frederick and John William, respectively. [18] Law and theological faculties at universities were often asked for opinions in these cases. [19]

As *oberster Lehnherr* of the German lands, the emperor himself was often forced to adjudicate these disputes when they could not be settled locally—a task he did not always perform graciously. Weary irritation can be imagined in Ferdinand II's voice as he reported having to make a decision in the contested adoption of primogeniture in Hesse-Kassel "only because of the divisions and errors of the quarrelsome world."[20] To assist him, he would name a commission made up of advisers and other princes of his choosing to serve as mediators. Establishing this body did not, however, suspend negotiations between spokesmen for the actual adversaries. It only meant that discussions went on at two levels rather than one.

Participants were well aware that such proceedings cost money. Imperial agents called upon to deal with the Saxon quarrel of 1566 tried to end the dispute as quickly as possible to keep down expenses.[21] But for all the time, effort, and revenue consumed in resolving these matters, settlements were usually short-lived. Even the most scrupulously evenhanded partition could not foresee all the contingencies that might spark another intradynastic squabble. The small-mindedness of it all echoes through the titles of some suits that came before the imperial aulic council in Vienna—"Hesse-Cassel contra Hesse-Cassel" or, morphologically yet more absurd, "Hessen-Darmbstadt vs. Hessen-Darmstatt"![22]

The personal lives of princes themselves were not immune to the upheavals inherent in territorial divisions. When lands fell (as they often did) into the hands of other members of a dynasty, either through death or other causes, new rulers sometimes took the opportunity to install their own appointees. Such a turn of events posed problems not only for bureaucrats who lost their jobs, but for members of the dynasty still living in and from the principality. Following a complicated and acrimonious suit over claims he made on his dead cousin's court in Weimar, Elector August of Saxony acquired some control over that establishment in 1573. He immediately began reorganizing the ducal bureaucracy. The late duke's widow, Dorothy Susanna, was beside herself with distress. She feared that August would remove councillors who had any knowledge of the ducal land division of 1572, thereby putting her minor sons at a serious disadvantage should they need advice on these matters in the future.[23] Real administrative chaos was avoided in these divisions only because court personnel were usually handed around rather than dismissed. Thus, new governments usually had some experienced hands to call upon.[24]

Partible inheritance complicated territorial legal affairs as well. Archives were prized possessions in these divisions since exclusive control of them could be tactically crucial in future disputes. Proving that Hesse-Homburg had claims against Hesse-Darmstadt was a far more challenging task than the jurist John Jacob Moser had expected. Hesse-Darmstadt had papers specifying rights agreed upon in a division between the branches in 1622–1623; the Homburg line did not have access to them. Not all families guarded their records so jealously, but using them could be cumbersome. A pact in the house of Anhalt in 1635 assigned its documents to the eldest brother with the understanding that the younger princes could copy from them. After Duke Frederick William I (1562–1602) of Saxony-Weimar created a separate regime for his sons in what became Saxony-Altenburg in 1603, legal records apparently stayed in Frederick William's capital. In the event that cases once litigated in Weimar were reopened in Altenburg, both courts were to keep abreast of one another's rulings to maintain judicial symmetry. If necessary, Weimar was to supply relevant materials. It also continued to hear all appeals in feudal questions since it remained the central repository for such matters.[25]

But the effects of partible inheritance were felt far beyond princes and their households. The integrity of universities—their capital, faculties, and endowments—was sometimes at stake in territorial partitions. A bitterly contested prize in the ducal Saxon land dispute of 1572 was the University of Jena. At issue was whether it should be governed in common by Duke John William, his nephews, and their guardian, Elector August, or be divided. After a false start or two by the imperial commissioners mediating the case, Maximilian II himself instructed that the university, its consistory and scholars be administered collectively, though only until John William's nephews came of age. A Hessian pact of 1628 gave Landgrave George of Hesse-Darmstadt the University of Marburg, its privileges, colleges, professors, tutors' homes, and all attached to these. Landgrave William V of Hesse-Kassel was left with the right to reactivate an old concession to establish a similar institution in Giessen. Whatever was not reserved for Landgrave George was to be split between them. This included, among other things, scholarships. Incomes drawn from properties Marburg owned were also to be divided with the stipulation that professors, tutors, and administrators who were not then working be paid what was owed them with a bonus![26]

As a single group, the booksellers and publishers of Leipzig probably suffered from partible inheritance more than most. Hard-hit by the wars of the sixteenth and seventeenth centuries and a depression that followed, they saw their trade dwindle. Competition from other Saxon lands made their plight even worse. By imperial law, publishers could operate only in cities that were princely residences, university towns, and sizeable commercial centers. As territorial divisions created fresh Saxon ducal establishments, printing, publishing, and sales outlets multiplied as well. New rulers often encouraged these undertakings by freeing them from taxes levied on the older concerns in Leipzig. Housing and salary concessions were sometimes further inducements offered to fledgling establishments.[27]

Even Protestantism, the very thing that encouraged these territorial divisions, was not immune to the troubles they provoked. Where territorial differences gave rise to sectarian ones, said John William of Saxony-Weimar, religion was especially ill served since "no one can serve two contradictory masters at the same time, and recognize and respect them as patrons."[28] Administrative responsibilities were often blurred, opening the way to misunderstanding and outright hostility. A Lutheran superintendent of Darmstadt thought himself competent to forbid a court preacher in Homburg from delivering the sermon at the funeral of the local landgrave's wife. Predictably, the Homburg clergyman objected sharply to such interference.[29] Protestant laity often resented confessional changes made simply to accommodate dynastic reshufflings. Should a Calvinist ruler come to a land once governed by a Lutheran, major changes in ceremony and teaching were in the offing, especially in the sixteenth century. When Elector Ludwig VI of the Palatine, a Lutheran, acquired Neustadt, which had been in the hands of his Calvinist brother, John Casimir (1543–1592), he immediately dismissed about five hundred of the church and school personnel, some of them forcibly. Four hundred pupils allegedly protested adoption of the new catechism that they expected to have to follow.[30]

Efforts to reconcile confessional differences within houses and their territories, however well meaning, led to weary indifference to all such distinctions among the faithful at large. In 1635, for example, the four branches of Anhalt tried to bring some uniformity into the ceremonial observed in their various lands. Divided between Calvinism and Lutheranism, all had employed the organ differently in their territorial churches. Lutheran Anhalt-Zerbst had used the instrument from the beginning of the Reformation. Anhalt-Cöthen had done away with it from 1596 to 1620. In the latter year, they began again "by special order of the prince." Dessau and Bernburg had not heard it from the beginning of their reform. The latter two principalities had to be brought into conformity with the first two or the other way around. All of this, according to the councillors of Anhalt-Zerbst struggling with the question, left the impression that "in these lands someone has to be reforming something all the time." In their opinion, ceremonial changes confused and angered the public far more than doctrinal revisions or inconsistencies, and they urged the princes to think the whole matter over very seriously.[31] The question was dropped from most versions of the family compact in which it was to appear.

German princes knew well that partible inheritance affected their lands and peoples adversely. In 1566, John William of Saxony-Weimar and his councillors rehearsed at length the negative impact such divisions had on the common welfare, justice, universities, schools, and "poor elderly church personnel, their widows and orphans."[32] Where rational stewardship of resources and promotion of the stature of the house were concerned, the princes had also long recognized that primogeniture was a desirable inheritance custom. Emperor Maximilian I toyed with the idea of introducing the practice in his family as he considered raising the Habsburg Austrian patrimony to a kingdom. Reconfirming primogeniture in his testament of 1578, Albert V of Bavaria cited the economic burdens to the Bavarian lands caused by too many reigning princes. Territorial divisions, he observed, encouraged dynastic division, all of which weakened "the reputation of our ancient princely house."[33] From the Lutheran side, Landgrave William IV of Hesse-Kassel was eloquent on the subject when he ordered the practice in his testament of 1576. Regarding himself as the prime victim of Philip of Hesse's partition, William did not want to repeat the same mistake with his two sons. Primogeniture, he asserted, would enable a prince to bear his duties, both local and imperial, more easily, defend himself more effectively, mete out justice more evenhandedly, and avoid the humiliating loss of reputation he had suffered when his father had split the Hessian patrimony.[34]

Through the centuries, however, and especially during the Reformation era, these were but a few of the princely considerations involved in personal and dynastic decisions. Indeed, such matters were often secondary to other concerns, religious precepts in particular. So secondary were they, in fact, that rulers refused to see how often partible inheritance failed to meet its stated goals. Partible inheritance had certainly never fulfilled the hope that brothers would live more harmoniously, one with the other. Divided inheritance and paternal admonitions to treat their stepbrothers well did not dispose the sons of Philip of Hesse's first marriage any more kindly toward the issue of his second wife. Indeed, the former could not "stand" the latter, according to Landgrave Ernest of Hesse-Rheinfels, Philip's grandson. The first set of siblings looked upon the second as the issue of a concubine, an opinion grounded in Ernest's belief that polygamy had not been carried over from the Old Testament to the New.[35] A father's decision to split his inheritance frequently angered firstborn sons as much as it pleased his brothers. Such hostility often endured a lifetime. Only filial piety persuaded Landgrave William IV of Hesse-Kassel to swallow his distress when his father partitioned his holdings.[36]

Others could not contain their resentment so manfully. When Elector Frederick III of the Palatine transferred the Amberg residence of his eldest son, Ludwig, to a junior brother, John Casimir (1543–1592), the former read this as one more sign that the younger man was indeed his father's favorite child.[37] Following the split between Hesse-Darmstadt and Hesse-Darmstadt-Homburg in 1622, Landgrave Frederick of Homburg agreed to pay the senior line a sum semiannually at the Frankfurt fair according to a rate established with the estates of Darmstadt in 1623. As late as 1692, Darmstadt was lodging formal complaints about the quality of the currency with which Homburg was meeting its obligation. Disputes over responsibilities for quartering troops were never resolved.[38] Even the Ernestine Saxons, who had perhaps invested partible inheritance with its heaviest moral freight, admitted that the custom had led to great quarreling among them.[39]

But knowing that partible inheritance was incompatible with the well-being of one's territories was one thing; remedying the situation through the introduction of primogeniture was quite another. That the overwhelming majority of German princes had by 1700 accepted the rule of the firstborn is clear—as is the fact that the change took place in a relatively short time. In 1650 the custom was relatively rare among Germany's Protestant rulers. Fifty years later, it was common. If religious values helped perpetuate partible inheritances, as this essay has argued, were they modified or altogether abandoned in order for this new development to take place? Should the response to this question be affirmative, the view that confession, regardless of content, was a major instrument in the consolidation of the German territorial state can no longer stand unqualified. This is of particular relevance for Lutheranism, until recently deemed the archexample of the close relationship between confessional reform and the growth of princely power.

Within the latter half of the seventeenth century, what changed the minds of German princes concerning primogeniture? What forced them to reassess attitudes that for centuries had guided them in family and territorial matters? Most evidence leads to the banal but inevitable conclusion that the economic and political consequences of the Thirty Years' War played a decisive role. More than any event, this protracted conflict persuaded even the most stubborn defenders of partible inheritance that the custom threatened dynastic survival itself.[40]

If nothing else, the hostilities between 1618 and 1648 made it clear that territorial divisions did not insure family harmony. For some princes, the battle was not only against foreign invaders, such as the Swedes, or a struggle for confessional survival. It was also an extension of the intrafamilial rivalries brought on by disputes over territorial divisions. Sides were sometimes chosen chiefly on these grounds, larger issues playing only a secondary role. Embroiled in a dispute over the testament of the landgrave of Hesse-Kassel-Marburg who had died childless in 1604, Hesse-Kassel and much smaller Hesse-Darmstadt fought in opposite camps during the Thirty Years' War, each hoping to resolve their local differences to their own advantage. Thus, a dynastic civil war brought further burdens to an area where Gustavus Adolphus and imperial troops clashed as well.[41]

But it was not only the belief that partible inheritance fostered princely harmony to which the war gave the lie. More seriously, it challenged the notion of princely equality upon which partible inheritance, indeed, the German dynastic system itself, was based. The conflict made it painfully clear that though in theory one prince was as representative of his family as another, individual territorial economies did not permit each to defend the interests of his house with equal effectiveness in periods of great crisis. The various lines of Anhalt, whose lands suffered grave financial dislocations during the war, grasped this quickly.

According to earlier agreements, members of that house were supposed to redistribute income among themselves so that their revenues would be almost the same—despite very considerable differences in the potential wealth of their holdings. Once the war came, the four princes, August, Ludwig, John Casimir (1596–1660), and George Aribert (d. 1677), resolved to contribute equally to the military effort as well. By 1637, however, John Casimir observed that each of their chief towns did not have equal resources at their disposal. His own residence of Dessau was racked by plague and other diseases. Half its houses, as he told it, were standing empty, and the situation was even worse in the outlying districts.[42] Efforts among the men to come to an understanding often failed; the electors of Saxony, Brandenburg, indeed, the emperor himself, were called upon to mediate among them. Some accord was finally established; yet the experience of the house showed that however praiseworthy and dynastically sound equality among brothers was, it had done much to undermine family harmony and territorial welfare.[43]

This war, along with the Turkish and French conflicts during the latter third of the century, sensitized the princes to the relationship between economic well-being and political survival in a deep and lasting way. By the end of the century, various dukes of Saxony were grumbling about increases in their obligations to the empire. Not all of their complaints were rhetorical.[44] Paragraph 180 of the Final Imperial Recess of 1654 committed territorial estates to the upkeep of fortresses and garrisons belonging to the estates of the empire as a whole.[45]

But perhaps the greatest reason for the princes to have developed a new awareness of the need for sound management of dynastic resources was the change in their territorial position finally acknowledged in the Peace of Westphalia. Now sovereign in their own lands, their courts took on the trappings of monarchy and sophistication, all of which was costly. The expenses of court life reached new and startling heights, as typified by the establishment of Ernest August of Braunschweig-Hannover. In 1678–79, his treasury recorded an annual payout of 304,671 *Taler,* 15 *Groschen,* and 3 *Pfennig.* In 1692–93, his expenses ran to 991,633 *Taler,* 8 *Groschen,* 3 *Pfennig;* and in 1697–98, 655,200 *Taler,* 23 *Groschen,* and 1-2/7 *Pfennig.* This last sum was much lower than the previous year, but still markedly higher than twenty years earlier. The breakdown of costs at his court in part explain the increase. Clothing his personnel before he became an elector or seriously pursued the office required only 2,955 *Taler,* 4 *Groschen,* 6 *Pfennig* in 1678–79. As his ambitions grew, so did his outlay for dress. In 1697–98 the cost of adorning his household grew to 9,208 *Taler,* 8 *Groschen,* 2 *Pfennig* and stayed approximately at that level the following year. Noted for a lavish kitchen, Ernest August spent ever-increasing sums in that area as well. In 1678–79, *"Küchengang"* came to 45,252 *Taler,* 25 *Groschen,* 3 *Pfennig.* In 1692–93, without any apparent major consolidation of budget categories, *"Hofstadt und Küche"* came to 105,717 *Taler,* 19 *Groschen,* 4 *Pfennig;* and in 1697–98, a staggering 126,498 *Taler,* 23 *Groschen,* 4-1/4 *Pfennig.* In 1696, Ernest August laid out 350,000 *Taler* for personnel, building projects, and the like—50 percent of his entire income.

The courts in Dresden and Brandenburg did the same, though in the case of Brandenburg, its incomes were substantially higher.[46]

A signal mark of sovereignty was the possession of a standing army. Not only Brandenburg came out of the seventeenth century with that innovation. Maximilian I of Bavaria established such a force, as did electoral Saxony. Hannover created one as early as 1651; Ernest August continued the practice, as well as contributing to local militias. All of this cost him around 500,000 *Taler* yearly. Indeed, five out of every hundred among his subjects were in the standing army, as opposed to militarized Prussia where the figure was 3.7 per hundred.[47]

To support all this, the reorganization of domestic economies became the motto of the day. Where this was impossible or did not yield hoped-for revenues, princes frequently became clients of richer foreign powers, making their claim to genuine sovereignty palpably absurd. Hannover was able to pay for its armies only through French subsidies and the sale of mercenaries, especially to Venice. When in need of funds, the electors of Saxony turned sometimes to Louis XIV, and sometimes to his archrival, the emperor in Vienna, depending upon who made the most advantageous offer.[48]

The time of the small state had come to an end and with it thoroughgoing partible inheritance. Even in cases where divisions had not been scrupulously equal, poverty had been spread rather than wealth enhanced. Such was the gloomy conclusion of Duke John George of Saxony-Eisenach (1634–1686) in his testament of November 30, 1685. Experience had taught him that when a young prince received only a few regalia and some territorial incomes with which to finance courts, administrations, or chancellories, resources dwindled quickly. Eisenach and Sayn, for example, were inadequate to such pretensions. No house, in his view, could long survive under such circumstances or enjoy all the dignities, honors, and rights due it. Nor could it satisfactorily meet its duties to the empire as whole.[49] His counterpart in Brandenburg-Prussia, Elector Frederick III, soon to become King Frederick I, pointed openly to the Wettin lands as an argument against conferring any principalities upon a cadet line of his own house. Such a practice, he vowed, "would inevitably bring with it the ruin of the house. I will only cite the example of Electoral Saxony and warn all my posterity with it."[50]

As the Protestant princes reassessed their political and economic positions, they also changed their religious views. The attitudes toward marriage and sexual morality, once closely tied to their faith, were affected as well. This development too was an epiphenomenon of the Thirty Years' War. Modern scholarship in general has documented a decline in religious fervor and the increased prominence of secular interests that appeared during and after the conflict. Confessional distinctions lost much of their edge of importance. The brutalities of war left many with no greater goal than finding personal happiness, an aim to which even Protestants made some accommodation. The high moral ideals of the Reformation receded markedly in this atmosphere, a condition noted unhappily by many pastors of the era. By the beginning of the eighteenth century, these views reached systematic philosophical expression in Leibniz's *Monadology*, which hypothesized an entire universe with no other purpose than the felicitous interaction of its component units—the so-called monads.[51]

What was once so compatible—dynastic strategy and confessional conviction—came asunder. Different approaches to the perpetuation of one's house emerged and had little in common with the nuptial idealism of the Reformation. Great numbers of children, once a valued asset for both house and faith, now seemed daunting burdens. Eisenach and Sayn could not support a whole household of princes, confessed Duke John George. Adolph Frederick of Mecklenburg advised his sons not to hurry with marriage. If they decided to take wives, he urged them to calculate whether their principalities and other incomes could sustain their offspring adequately. Repeated divisions of family incomes, heretofore an inexorable by-product of children, would weaken their lands even further. Seven sons through two marriages, though a blessing, said Count Christian of Waldeck (1635–1706), were just too many to maintain through territorial divisions, a practice that he now called ruinous.[52]

A far more cold-blooded view of wedlock accompanied this newly somber appraisal of large families. The same Adolph Frederick of Mecklenburg now counseled his sons, if they must marry, to pay some attention to the size of the dowry that a bride might bring "in order that our princely house be augmented."[53] As his life came to a close, Duke August of Saxony-Weissenfels (1614–1680) had much the same advice for his eight sons from two marriages. He did draw the line, however, at Catholic or Calvinist brides for the men. It was not the piety of the daughter of the elector of Brandenburg that attracted Prince Karl of Mecklenburg-Güstrow (1664–1688); rather, he hoped to lighten his territorial arrears with the large dowry that he thought she would have. A governorship in the Hohenzollern lands to which he expected an appointment would help as well.

The counts of Reuss, who once prized virtue and *Ebenbürtigkeit* in their wives, now grew cautious about marrying at all. Before doing so, they agreed that they would give very serious thought to the material consequences of the step. How far would they be forced into debt? How often would they have to divide their already shrunken principalities among future offspring? What kind of fiscal pressures would their daughters' dowries impose upon their lands?[54]

The more German princes treated marriage as an economic issue, the more cynically they approached it. Prince Frederick August of Braunschweig-Hannover believed that the custom needed only three things to make it happy—honorableness, utility, and "pleasure" (*le délicieux*). Nothing in this world being perfect, he was willing to settle for the first two. Through an alliance with a great house, he hoped that his own would profit.[55] His attitude bespoke a general relaxation of moral norms at the German Protestant courts during the second half of the seventeenth century. Taking as their sexual role model Louis XIV, the embodiment of princely power for his age, the empire's rulers often outdid the French monarch himself in their range of amatory adventures. Here and there, defenders of princely polygamy appeared. In 1689, for example, a certain Böger, librarian to the Elector Palatine, justified the practice. One pastor Kornbeck of Neckarweihingen upheld the marriage of Eberhard IV Ludwig of Württemberg (1676–1733) to one of his mistresses, even as he reminded the duke that he had a lawfully wedded duchess.

Such attitudes contrasted sharply with those from a century earlier when the German princes, almost to a man, publicly condemned the tormented Philip of Hesse's bigamy.[56] The Lutheran church in Germany certainly opposed such practices, but often futilely. Reverend Philippi of the *Sophienkirche* in Dresden was exiled for conscientiously chiding the most notorious philanderer of his age, August the Strong. Samuel Urlsperger, court preacher in Stuttgart, was actually sentenced to death for similar moralizing.[57]

It was not only in matters of marriage and sexual morality that Germany's Protestant princes subordinated their religious values to purely economic ones. Their confessional loyalties suffered as well. The simple desire to better themselves produced many conversions to Catholicism in the seventeenth century. In electoral Saxony, the very heartland of Lutheranism, August the Strong adopted the faith of Rome to accommodate his new subjects when he became king of Poland in 1697. The opportunity to marry into the imperial house influenced two princesses from Braunschweig to become Catholics, thereby rendering them acceptable in Vienna.[58]

Thus did the religious and moral preoccupations of the Reformation fade in the face of political and economic pressures. And it was under these same pressures that Germany's Protestant rulers followed the example of their Catholic counterparts and adopted primogeniture. Once scorned for its worldliness, the custom now seemed the only avenue to rational management of dynastic incomes and possessions. Appanages, of course, endured, but, as we have already seen, they were a pale version of partible inheritance. Some princes were still deeply troubled in their consciences by the step. While admitting that the rule of the firstborn was needed in order "to maintain the lustre of the house of Waldeck," Count Christian (1635–1706) of that dynasty swore by God and his "Christian conscience" that he was equally well disposed toward each of his seven male offspring.[59] John George of Saxony-Eisenach justified the practice before his Maker himself in his testament, hoping that He would bestow His blessings on a measure that the duke continued to insist was taken "not with regard for worldly splendor and pomp, but for the more constant preservation of principalities and lands given to us, for the true propagation of his divine word, as well as for the management of beloved justice, service of the fatherland, and successful administration."[60] Some were openly disappointed that partible inheritance was no longer viable. Even as Duke Ernest Ludwig of Saxony-Coburg-Meiningen (1672–1724) granted that dividing resources had not brought uniformly positive results to his family, he clearly regretted having to abandon the practice.[61]

Deeply rooted beliefs and habits of thought lingered on. As late as 1695, the theological faculty at the university of Wittenberg maintained that God himself would be displeased by parents binding children to continue the rule of primogeniture in their houses.[62] Although compelled to adopt the rule of the firstborn, many princes continued to search out scriptural justification for their actions. True to the pious traditions of his house, Frederick I of Saxony-Gotha (1646–1691) urged his disinherited sons to accept their lot "according to their Christian consciences" for the good of their house. As he saw it, divine law sanctioned his action.[63] Some of his contemporaries explained this view in far more detail. It was, of course, an injunction of the decalogue to honor one's parents. John George of Saxony-Eisenach urged his second son to accept primogeniture out of "sonly obedience," which would be pleasing to God. Ernest of Saxony-Coburg-Meiningen gruffly ordered his children to accept the custom or suffer the consequences of violating this biblical commandment.[64] Duchess, later Electress, Sophia of Braunschweig-Hannover reluctantly advised her younger sons to accept their father's introduction of primogeniture into their line on the grounds that both divine and human law ordered submission to one's parents.[65] Other rulers noted that David and Solomon had handed on their thrones to only one of their sons. Both kings, it was emphasized, were strong protectors of their peoples. The subsequent territorial division under Rehoboam, leading to the formation of Israel and Judea, was now brought forth to exemplify the disadvantages of such practices.[66]

But for all of these devout rationalizations, Germany's princes were now thinking in far more secular terms about themselves and dynastic advantage. Indeed, several princes felt no need to find scriptural justifications for adopting primogeniture. Rather, they spoke only of the dangers that partible inheritance posed to their houses and others. Maximilian I of Bavaria's admonitions about the preeminent need for a strong state had taken root in the Protestant world as well, but with a difference. Whereas the Wittelsbach had argued that only through a financially sound Bavaria could Catholicism be defended, late seventeenth-century Lutherans and Calvinists worried only about the survival of their houses.

Among the most eloquent Protestants to confront the primogeniture question was Ernest August of Braunschweig-Hannover. Openly acknowledging the importance of raw military and economic power, the duke had many reasons for concern about the position of his territories and foreign designs upon them. Sweden's acquisition of Bremen and Verden through the Treaty of Westphalia made his lands vulnerable to attack from that quarter. Nor was Ernest August without ambitions of his own. If the Swedes could be dislodged, he was anxious to have Bremen and Verden for himself.[67]

Denmark and the bishopric of Münster, however, had the same designs. In the 1680s, the Danes began harassing Hamburg, and the elector of Brandenburg, Frederick William, became partners with the east Frisian estates in an African trading company. Ernest August felt more threatened than ever.[68] In his eyes, and in those of his librarian and adviser, the polymath Gottfried William Leibniz, there was only one way to avoid being crushed in this territorial crunch as well as to reestablish the glories of the house of Welf that had been in eclipse since the defeat of Henry the Lion by Barbarossa in the twelfth century. The solution was to become an elector. In order to do so, Ernest August had to meet the territorial requirements of the Golden Bull and make his lands indivisible. The introduction of primogeniture was unavoidable.[69]

Ernest August had already shown that his Lutheran heritage would not stand in the way of ambition. In 1677 he had explored in Rome the possibility of converting to Catholicism if the pope would allow his family to administer the bishoprics of Osnabrück and Hildesheim as long as the line continued. The *ius patronatus* of Corvey was also to remain in the hands of his branch of the dynasty, and he himself would be allowed to dispense its benefices to his numerous male progeny.[70]

The scheme never materialized, but it demonstrated that in matters of confession, family, and interests of state, the duke and Leibniz were well matched. As indifferent to distinctions of faith as his employer, especially where relations among polities were concerned, the philosopher was also a firm opponent of partible inheritance: "For it is even also a fundamentally false and destructive opinion that peoples and states are private possessions of a reigning prince, who can divide and bequeath them like horses, landed properties and other [forms of] wealth. That is contrary to all law and reason."[71]

Such utilitarian and naturalistic defenses of primogeniture echoed or anticipated wider changes taking place in thinking about dynastic relations and family relations in general throughout the empire. In his *De jure naturae et gentium,* first published in 1672, the jurist Samuel Pufendorf argued that the union of husband and wife had as its sole purpose the perpetuation of human society through procreation. Though this view was not wholly at odds with Christian opinion, the frame of reference within which Pufendorf developed it was societal, not theological. He furthermore regarded siring offspring as inhumane if they could not be cared for properly.[72]

As the religious significance of children waned, so did the attachment to partible inheritance. In 1713 an anonymous memorandist in Vienna claimed that the rule of the firstborn was a matter of simple logic. Since a throne could not be divided, only one man could succeed to it. The custom of all peoples, he contended somewhat airily, was the observance of primogeniture.[73] Ernest August of Hannover was more eloquent: "We cannot organize our council and decrees according to affection, but must do it according to the principle of the state. The consolidation of the principalities under one administration would be a necessary and unavoidable thing. The person to whom we leave a government after our death is a matter which does not depend upon our will, but must follow nature, and to whom that goes through order of birth, primacy, and advantage, even we ourselves cannot take that from him."[74]

It was incumbent on reasonable men, by whom Ernest August meant his male offspring, to accept this decision. He advised that they might be happier if they turned to conducting themselves well rather than brooding over the injustice of having one among them receive the bulk of the family wealth.[75] In asking imperial confirmation of this change in inheritance customs of his dynasty, Ernest August pointed out that thrones were neither inherited privately nor managed for one's personal use.[76] Rather, they were instruments for enhancing public welfare.

Such views were strikingly reminiscent of those held by Justus Lipsius, whom we previously encountered at the beginning of the seventeenth century in Catholic Bavaria. The reason is not hard to find. Lipsius had won a wide following among German princes and their advisers. August II the Strong of Saxony was tutored by John Frederick Reinhard, who personally revised Lipsius's *Six Books of Politics or Civil Doctrine,* bringing the work out in 1702. More significant in Ernest August's case, however, is the fact that the center of Lipsian thought in seventeenth-century Germany was the Saxon University of Jena, which boasted Leibniz as its most famous contemporary student.[77]

Such views were thoroughly consonant with enhancing the power of the secular state and the prince who directed it. They were altogether compatible with the introduction of primogeniture, long recognized as a means of improving a prince's domestic resources. They were, however, hostile to the small principality, the venerable staple of partible inheritance. Veit Ludwig von Seckendorff, a bitter critic of German *Kleinstaaterei* after much experience with the practice in Saxony-Gotha, would pick up Leibniz's maxim that war, military affairs, and economic policies that supported these activities were the key functions of the state.[78] Few, if any, of Germany's small principalities were equipped to handle such responsibilities.

The law of primogeniture was a prescription that governed what heretofore had been a ruler's private behavior, even if his personal inclinations prompted him to do otherwise: "We cannot organize our council and decrees according to affection." The custom required self-discipline from princes in the fullest Lipsian sense. Some did not like it. Adolf Frederick of Mecklenburg-Schwerin noted in his testament of 1654 that he was dutifully observing a form of primogeniture that existed in his house, despite his eldest sons's having "deeply and frequently offended us."[79]

Whether the Protestant princes came to this sober approach to their families and resources because of reasoned insight into the conflict between religious values and political self-interest or simply because the hold of religious principles on their imaginations had weakened is difficult to say. The troubled consciences of Christian of Waldeck or the Saxon dukes upon adopting primogeniture argues for the first position; the readiness of Protestants to become Catholics for the sake of better livings or the carefree promiscuity of August the Strong of electoral Saxony supports the second. But neither point has been the fundamental issue of this essay. What has been under examination here is the widely accepted proposition that religious discipline and political discipline were mutually supportive in the consolidation of princely absolutism in early modern Germany. Clearly that relationship was more ambiguous than even current scholarship would allow.

This is not to say that in enforcing the confessional norms demanded by both the Protestant and Catholic reforms, German rulers did not increase their control over the lives of their subjects and realize long-standing political and administrative goals. But to learn this is not to exhaust the topic of the relationship between religion and politics in early modern Germany, as many seem ready to believe. When, as we have done here, we turn to the question of the impact that confession had upon the husbanding of dynastic resources, so essential to the growth and survival of the territorial state, a quite different picture appears. Catholic princes, hard pressed in the defense of their faith and mindful that they needed to preserve the means to carry out that mission, behaved far more flexibly when managing their holdings. The abandonment of partible inheritance and creation of territorial unity came much more easily to the Wittelsbach and Habsburg lands than to many of their Protestant counterparts. Because they still had a far richer assortment of ecclesiastical positions in which to place younger sons, rulers loyal to the church of Rome were far better situated to observe the moral imperatives of their faith, even as they acted to political advantage. Put another way, they found it far easier to reconcile confession with reason of state.

In the Protestant camp, however, Lutheran and Calvinist alike struggled with the same issue but found their faith of little assistance. Rather, it placed unanticipated burdens on dynastic resources. When finally the majority of Protestant German princes did accept the primacy of reason of state and primogeniture that went with it, they did so with far less religious purpose than had the Habsburgs and the Wittelsbachs. Protestantism had done as much to block territorial unity as to foster it.

But the story of Germany's Protestant rulers and their acceptance of primogeniture has even further ramifications for current historiography. The picture we now have of the territorial state and its development is one that pits the German prince against other interests, usually his estates, either singly or collectively.[80] Both seek to bend one another to their own purposes, to "discipline" one another, as it were. When the German territorial prince succeeds, as he frequently did in the seventeenth and eighteenth centuries, the political structure that emerges is called "absolutism." Where the prince was forced to major compromise, it is called "dualism." In either case, the system is the result of a clash between two or more discrete sets of interests. The prince and his administration work to school his subjects in his economic, military and confessional purposes. The subjects labor mightily to protect local interests. So great is the mutual impact of these endeavors that early modern society as a whole becomes the object of study rather than what is rather dismissively termed "political-dynastic historiography."[81]

But as we watch Germany's Protestant princes struggle with the contrary dictates of religious principle and political interests, we see that dynastic history is also a part of the modernizing process. In resisting the rule of the firstborn, German rulers were not confronting some external opponent. Rather, in overcoming their moral reservations to primogeniture, which the Protestant Reformation had quickened, they were forcing themselves and their families to rethink their territorial roles. The entrenchment of princely absolutism changed internal dynastic relations as much as it did the relationship between a ruler and his subjects at large.

Ultimately, we are left with something like a paradox in all of this, if history can be said to generate paradoxes at all. Religious persuasions such as Calvinism and Lutheranism, which made self-discipline so central to spiritual development, should not have been so troublesome when it came to preserving the very states upon which their survival as confessions rested. But if historical events are rarely the result of one factor, they may have many, and contradictory, consequences as well. This is all the more true when the "events" in question are complex systems of religious belief. The symmetry between ideas and institutions may often be partial at best. Those historians whose intellectual satisfactions come in establishing clear and direct lines of development are generally uncomfortable with such findings. For those who discover such incompatibility at first hand and must then resolve its consequences, the experience is unhappier still.

NOTES

Introduction

1. Werner Näf, "Frühformen des 'modernen Staates' im Spätmittelalter," *Historische Zeitschrift* 171 (1951): 229, 235, 239; Heinrich Otto Meisner, "Staats- und Regierungsformen in Deutschland im 16. Jahrhundert," *Archiv für öffentliches Recht* 77 (1952): 225–40; Theodore Rabb, *The Struggle for Stability in Early Modern Europe* (New York: Oxford University Press, 1975), 71; Geoffrey Parker and Lesley M. Smith, eds., *The General Crisis of the Seventeenth Century* (London: Routledge and Kegan Paul, 1978), 6, 15–16; Max Braubach, "Vom westfälischen Frieden bis zur französischen Revolution," in Bruno Gebhardt, *Handbuch der deutschen Geschichte*, 9th ed., 4 vols. (Stuttgart: Union/Klett, 1970–76, 2:253; Quentin Skinner, *The Foundations of Modern Political Thought*, 2 vols. (Cambridge: Cambridge University Press, 1978), 2:15; Friedrich Meinecke, "Luther über christliches Gemeinwesen und christlichen Staat," *Historische Zeitschrift* 121 (1920): 21; Ludwig Zimmerman, "Moderne Staatsbildung in Deutschland," in *Herrschaft und Staat in Mittelalter*, Wege der Forschung, no. 2 (Darmstadt: Wissenschaftliche Buchgesellschaft, 1950), 387; Horst Dreitzel, *Protestantischer Aristotelismus und absoluter Staat: Die "Politica" des Henning Arnisaeus* (Wiesbaden: Steiner, 1970), 363; Gerhard Oestreich, *Neostoicism and the Early Modern State,* ed. Brigitta Oestreich and H. F. Koenigsberger, trans. David McLintock (Cambridge: Cambridge University Press, 1982), 225.

2. William L. Shirer, *The Rise and Fall of the Third Reich* (New York: Simon and Schuster, 1960), 236–37; Marc Raeff, *The Well-Ordered Police State: Social and Institutional Change through Law in the Germanies and Russia, 1600–1800* (New Haven: Yale University Press, 1983), 26 and passim.

3. An exceptionally useful compilation on this question is James D. Tracy, ed. *Luther and the Modern State in Germany,* Sixteenth Century Essays and Studies, no. 7 (Kirksville, Mo.: Sixteenth Century Journal Publishers, 1986),

especially the essays be Heinz Schilling and Karlheinz Blaschke. See also Gerald Strauss, *Law, Resistance and the State: The Opposition to Roman Law in Reformation Germany* (Princeton: Princeton University Press, 1986), 234, 150–51, 237–38; Hartmut Lehmann, *Das Zeitalter des Absolutismus: Gottesgnadentum und Kriegsnot* (Stuttgart: Kohlhammer, 1980) 23–24, 33; Heinz Schilling, *Konfessionskonflikt und Staatsbildung: Eine Fallstudie über das Verhältnis von religiösem und sozialem Wandel in der Frühneuzeit am Beispiel der Grafschaft Lippe*. Quellen und Forschungen zur Reformationsgeschichte, no. 48 (Gütersloh: Mohn, 1980), 380–83; Volker Press, "Martin Luther und die sozialen Kräfte seiner Zeit," in *Luther und die politische Welt*, ed. Erwin Iserloh and Gerhard Müller. Historische Forschungen no. 9 (Wiesbaden: Steiner, 1984), 2.

4. Both quotations are found in Thomas A. Brady, Jr., "The Political Masks of Martin Luther," *History Today* 33 (November 1983): 27.

5. Schilling, *Konfessionskonflikt*, 35–36, 42–44, 361 *n*1; Lehmann, *Absolutismus*, 24, 33.

6. Strauss, *Law*, chap. 5 and p. 156.

7. Hermann Schulze, *Das Recht der Erstgeburt in den deutschen Fürstenhäusern und seine Bedeutung für die deutsche Staatsentwicklung* (Leipzig: Avenarius und Mendelsohn, 1851), 250.

8. Evelyn Cecil, *Primogeniture* (London: Murray, 1895), 122.

9. Ruth Altmann, *Landgraf Wilhelm V. von Hessen-Kassel im Kampf gegen Kaiser und Katholizismus 1633–1637* (Marburg: Elwert, 1938), 33–34; Braubach, "Vom westfälischen Frieden," 253; J. P. Cooper, "Patterns of Inheritance and Settlement by Great Landowners from the Fifteenth to the Eighteenth Centuries," in *Family and Inheritance: Rural Society in Western Europe 1200–1800*, ed. Jack Goody et al. (Cambridge: Cambridge University Press, 1976), 194.

10. Herbert Rowen, *The King's State: Proprietary Dynasticism in Early Modern France* (New Brunswick, N. J.: Rutgers University Press, 1980), 1; Eduard Sieber, *Die Idee des Kleinstaates bei den Deutschen des 18. Jahrhunderts in Frankreich und Deutschland* (Basel: Basler Bücherstube Kobers Buch und Kunsthandlung, A. G., 1920), 103 *n*1.

Chapter I: Men of Politics, Men of Faith

1. Gerhard Benecke, *Society and Politics in Germany 1500–1750* (London: Routledge and Kegan Paul, 1974), 162.

2. Schulze, *Erstgeburt*, 150, 152–53, 228.

3. Ralph Giesey, *The Juristic Basis of Dynastic Right to the French Throne*, Transactions of the American Philosophical Society, n.s., 51, pt. 5 (Philadelphia: American Philosophical Society, 1961): 8; J. E. A. Jolliffe, *The Constitutional History of Medieval England*, 3d ed. (London: Black, 1954),

183; Paul Viollet, *Histoire des institutions politiques et administratives de la France* (Paris: Larose et Forcal, 1900–03), 183; Andrew W. Lewis, *Royal Succession in Capetian France: Studies on Familial Order and the State* (Cambridge: Harvard University Press, 1981), 155, 157, 162, 181, 196.

4. Hermann Schulze, *Das Erb- und Familienrecht der deutschen Dynastien des Mittelalters* (Halle: Buchhandlung des Waisenhauses, 1871), 35, 41–42; Conrad Bornhak, *Deutsche Verfassungsgeschichte vom westfälischen Frieden an* (Stuttgart: Enke, 1934), 20.

5. Schulze, *Erstgeburt*, 242–43, 230, 232–33; Albert Werminghoff, *Der Rechtsgedanke von der Unteilbarkeit des Staates in der deutschen und brandenburg-preussischen Geschichte*, Hallische Universitätsreden, no. 1 (Halle: Niemeyer, 1915), 14; Wilhelm Klank, *Die Entwicklung des Grundsatzes der Unteilbarkeit und Primogenitur im Kurfürstentum Brandenburg* (Borna: Noske, 1908), 1–7, has the pertinent articles of the Golden Bull.

6. Theodore F. T. Plucknett, *Taswell-Langmead's English Constitutional History*, 11th ed. (London: Sweet and Maxwell, 1960), 475; Giesey, *Juristic Basis*, 8; Rowen, *King's State*, 24.

7. Schulze, *Erstgeburt*, 230.

8. Georg von Below, *Die Ursachen der Rezeption des römischen Rechts in Deutschland* (Munich: Oldenbourg, 1905), 119–20; Strauss, *Law*, 142; Cooper, "Patterns of Inheritance," in *Family and Inheritance*, ed. Goody et al., citing Richard Pipes, *Russia under the Old Regime*, 182; Georg Melchior Ludolf, *De introductione juris primogeniturae*, 3d ed. (Jena: Bielck, 1733), *Pars generalis*, 23.

9. William of Hesse to Count Ludwig of the Palatine, 28 December 1571, in *Briefe Friedrich des Frommen Kurfürsten von der Pfalz*, ed. August von Kluckhohn, 2 vols. in 3 (Braunschweig: Schwetschke, 1868–72), vol. 2, pt. 1:439.

10. Hermann Schulze, ed. *Die Hausgesetze der regierenden deutschen Fürstenhäuser*, 3 vols. (Jena: Fischer, 1862–83), vol. 1:6–24, 366–90, 224–40; vol. 2:8–34; vol. 3:14–73, 562–75. For a detailed picture of these divisions and their genealogical ramifications, see Wilhelm Karl Prinz zu Isenburg, *Europäische Stammtafeln: Stammtafeln zur Geschichte der europäischen Staaten*, n.s., ed. Detlev Schwennicke, 10 vols. (Marburg: Stargardt, 1980), vol. 1: table 25 (Bavaria); 15–16 (Austria); 43 (Saxony); 73–74 (Anhalt); 98–99, 104 (Hesse); 139–40 (Mecklenburg); 63, 65 (Braunschweig); 153–55, 159a–60 (Brandenburg).

11. Johann Heinrich Gelbke, *Herzog Ernst genannt der Fromme zu Gotha als Mensch und Regent*, 3 vols. in 1 (Gotha: Perthes, 1810), 1:176–77; Walter Pass, *Musik und Musiker am Hof Maximilians II*, Wiener Veröffentlichungen zur Musikwissenschaft (Tutzing: Schneider, 1980), 20:310; Cecil, *Primogeniture*, 122.

12. "Declaration of Archduke Leopold to Ferdinand II," 1623, in Victor von

Renner, "Die Erbteilung Kaiser Ferdinand II. mit seinen Brüdern," *Zeitschrift des Ferdinandeums für Tirol und Vorarlberg*, 3d ser., 18 (1873): 221. Cf. Felix Pischel, "Die Entwicklung der Zentralverwaltung in Sachsen-Weimar bis 1743," *Zeitschrift des Vereins für thüringische Geschichte und Altertumskunde*, n.s., 20 (1911): 240–41.

13. Veit Ludwig von Seckendorff, *Teutscher Fürstenstaat*, 5th ed. (Frankfurt am Main: Götzen, 1708), 171–72.

14. Copies of Maurice's third testament in Hessisches Staatsarchiv Marburg (hereafter Marburg SA), Bestand 4a, *Politische Akten nach Philipp dem Grossen: Abteilung a: Landgräfliche Personalien*, Repositur 38.1–38.5, no fol. no.

15. Otto von Heinemann, *Geschichte von Braunschweig und Hannover*, 2 vols. (Gotha: Perthes, 1884–86), 2:335–37, 355; Hermann Kunst, *Evangelischer Glaube und politische Verantwortung: Martin Luther als politischer Berater* (Stuttgart: Evangelischer Verlagswerk, 1976), 37.

16. [Franz von Krenner], *Der Landtag im Herzogthum Baiern vom Jahre 1514* (n.p: 1804), 299; Otto Stolz, *Geschichte des Landes Tirol* (Innsbruck: Tyrolia, 1955), 533.

17. Schulze, *Erstgeburt*, 341; Johann Jakob Moser, *Teutsches Staatsrecht*, 50 vols. (Leipzig und Ebersdorff im Vogtland: Vollrath, 1737–53), 14:431; Julius Ficker, *Vom Reichsfürstenstände: Forschungen zur Geschichte der Reichsverfassung zunächst im XII. und XIII. Jahrhunderte*, 2 vols. (Innsbruck: Wagner, 1861–1932), 1:265–66; Waldemar Domke, *Die Viril-Stimmen im Reichsfürstenrath von 1495–1654*, Untersuchungen zur deutschen Staats und Rechtsgeschichte, no. 11 (Breslau: Koebner, 1882), 139.

18. Werminghoff, *Rechtsgedanke*, 9.

19. Henry Julius von Braunschweig-Wolfenbüttel, "Tragoedia Hiehadbel. von einem ungeratenen Sohn welcher unmenschliche und unerhörte mordthaten begangen, auch endliche neben seinen mit consorten schrecklich und grewliche ende genomen hat," *Bibliothek des litterarischen Vereins in Stuttgart*, no. 36 (Tübingen: Litterarischer Verein, 1855), 374.

20. "Suasio ad primogenituram introducendam in domo Austriaca," Vienna, Haus-, Hof-, und Staatsarchiv (hereafter HHStA), Familienarchiv, *Familienakten* I.1, *Hausgesetze*, Karton 1, Konv. 1, fol. 15; Landgrave William of Hesse-Kassel to Count Ludwig of the Palatine, 28 December 1571, *Briefe Friedrich des Frommen*, ed. August Kluckhohn (Braunschweig: Schwetschke, 1868–72), vol. 3, pt. 1:440–41; Paul Haake, "Ein politisches Testament König Augusts des Starken," *Historische Zeitschrift* 87 (1901): 11. Duchess Sophia of Braunschweig-Hannover to Prince Frederick August, 14 January 1685, *Prinzenbriefe zum hannoverschen Primogeniturstreit 1685–1701*, ed. Anna Wendland, Quellen und Darstellungen zur Geschichte Niedersachsens, no. 46 (Hildesheim: Lax, 1937), 7; Prince Christian Henry to Electress Sophia of Hannover, 11 January 1699, ibid., p. 54.

21. Archduke Leopold to Archduke Charles, 7 November 1623, in Renner, "Erbteilung", 223; Archduke Leopold's Declaration to Ferdinand II, 10 November 1623, ibid., pp. 225–26.

22. Sigismund Peller, "Studies on Mortality since the Renaissance," pt. 2, *Bulletin of the History of Medecine* 21 (1947): 87; Georg Schnath, *Geschichte Hannovers im Zeitalter der neunten Kur und der englishchen Sukzession,* 2 vols. (Hildesheim: Lax, 1938–76), 1:736 *n*1.

23. Landgrave Ernest of Hesse-Kassel-Rheinfels to Gottfried Wilhelm von Leibniz, 1 February 1691, in Gottfried Wilhelm von Leibniz, *Allgemeiner politischer und historischer Briefwechsel,* 7 vols. in 8 (Darmstadt: Reidel/ Akademie, 1923–1970), 6:174.

24. Hans Sachs, "Comedia. Jacob mit seinem bruder Esaw," ed. Adelbert von Keller, *Bibliothek des litterarischen Vereins in Stuttgart,* no. 102 (Tübingen: Litterarischer Verein, 1870), 91–92; Schnath, *Geschichte Hannovers* 1:292–93.

25. Schulze, *Erstgeburt,* 327.

26. Christian von Rommel, *Geschichte von Hessen,* 10 vols. (Kassel: Perthes, 1820–58), 4:321. For sketches and copies of Landgrave Maurice's testament see Marburg SA, Bestand 4a, *Politische Akten nach Philipp dem Grossen,* Abteilung a: *Landgräfliche Personalien,* Paket 38.1–38.5

27. Klank, *Unteilbarkeit,* 19; Schulze, *Erstgeburt,* 404; Werminghoff, *Rechtsgedanke,* 18. The Great Elector's eventual heir, King Frederick I of Prussia, said that he was never able to confirm this account; see Richard Dietrich, ed., *Politische Testamente der Hohenzollern* (Munich: Deutscher Taschenbuch Verlag, 1981), 88.

28. Dorothy Susanna of Saxony-Weimar to Electress Anna, 20 April 1573, Vienna, HHStA, Reichskanzlei, *Kleinere Reichsstände, Sachsen-Gotha,* fasc. 441, no fol. no.

29. Schulze, *Hausgesetze* 3:277–78, and *Erstgeburt,* 336.

30. Krenner, *Landtag 1514,* 299.

31. Ibid., 456.

32. For example, Rowen, *King's State,* 1.

33. Schulze, *Erstgeburt,* 213, 222–23, 226; Ludolf, *De introductione, Pars generalis,* 8.

34. Testament of Duke George of Braunschweig-Lüneburg, 1641, in Ludolf, *De introductione,* appendix, fasc. 3, p. 72.

35. Paula Sutter Fichtner, "Dynastic Marriage in Sixteenth-Century Habsburg Diplomacy and Statecraft: An Interdisciplinary Approach," *American Historical Review* 21 (1976): 251.

36. Hans Sturmberger, "Die Anfänge des Bruderzwistes in Habsburg. Das Problem einer österreichischen Länderteilung nach dem Tod Maximilians II. und die Residenz des Erzherzogs Matthias in Linz," *Mitteilungen des oberösterreichischen Landesarchivs* 5 (1957): 170.

37. Schulze, *Hausgesetze* 2:57; Gelbke, *Herzog Ernst,* 3, documentary appendix: 119–47; Moser, *Staatsrecht* 12:474; Schulze, *Erstgeburt,* 246.

38. John William of Saxony-Weimar to Maximilian II, 5 July 1572, HHStA, Reichskanzlei, *Kleinere Reichsstände, Sachsen-Gotha,* fasc. 440, fol. 7. (The folio number means very little since the rest of the fascicle is largely unfoliated.) Frederick III's undated memorandum, ibid., fasc. 439, no fol. no.

39. Ferdinand Schrötter, *Abhandlungen aus dem österreichischen Staatsrecht und aus Freiheitsbriefen,* 5 vols. in 3 (Vienna: Krauss, 1762–66), 5:197.

40. Maximilian II to his commissioners, 3 May 1571, HHStA, Reichskanzlei, *Kleinere Reichsstände, Sachsen-Gotha,* fasc. 439, no fol. no.

41. Memorandum of Ferdinand III to the Imperial Aulic Council, 1650?, HHStA, Reichskanzlei, *Kleinere Reichsstände, Hessen-Cassel,* fasc. 156, fol. 669.

42. Bornhak, *Verfassungsgeschichte,* 22; Kunigunde's instructions to her representatives to Maximilian I, May–June? 1514, Krenner, *Landtag 1514,* 456.

43. For example, petition of Hesse-Kassel to the Emperor, HHStA, Reichskanzlei, *Kleinere Reichsstände, Hessen-Cassel,* fasc. 153, fol. 6; Hesse-Kassel to Hesse-Darmstadt, "Septem Questiones . . . ," 1650–52?, ibid., fasc. 156, fol. 193.

44. Gottlieb Krause, ed., *Urkunden,Aktenstücke und Briefe zur Geschichte der anhaltischen Lande und ihrer Fürsten unter dem Druck des 30 Jährigen Krieges,* 5 vols. (Leipzig: Dyk, 1861–66), 3:166.

45. Gottfried Müller, Chancellor of Anhalt-Dessau, Protocol on his discussion with Christian II of Anhalt-Bernburg, 15–16 December 1635, Krause, *Urkunden* 3:866–73; Christian of Anhalt-Bernburg? to his brothers, February 1635, ibid., p. 164.

46. Councillors of the Elector Palatine and the electors of Saxony and Brandenburg to Maximilian II, 5 August 1571, HHStA, Reichskanzlei, *Kleinere Reichsstände, Sachsen-Gotha,* fasc. 439, no fol. no.; Councillors of the Elector Palatine, etc., to Maximilian II, 26 October 1571, ibid., no fol. no.

47. Rosbeck to Maximilian II, 1572, HHStA, Reichskanzlei, *Kleinere Reichsstände, Sachsen-Gotha,* fasc. 440, no fol. no.; Elector August I of Saxony to Maximilian II, 5 August 1571, ibid., fasc. 439, no fol. no.

48. Imperial commissioners to Maximilian II, 5 August 1572, HHStA, Reichskanzlei, *Kleinere Reichsstände, Sachsen-Gotha,* fasc. 440, no fol. no.; Maximilian II to his commissioners, 8 December 1572, ibid., no fol. no.

49. HHStA, Reichskanzlei, *Kleinere Reichsstände, Hessen-Cassel,* fasc. 157, no fol. no.

50. Krause, *Urkunden* 3:165–66.

51. *Saalfeldisches Recess-buch: die Verfassung des herzoglichen Sachsen-Gothäischen*

Gesammthauses die in demselben vorgenommenen Erbtheilungen, vornehmlich aber die . . . Sachsen-Coburg-Saalfeldischen Gerechtsamen betreffend (Coburg: Uhl, 1783), 67–68.

52. Archduke Leopold to Father Lamormaini, 27 July 1625, in B. Dudik, ed., "Correspondenz Kaisers Ferdinand II. und seiner erlauchten Familie mit P. Martinus Becanus und P. Wilhelm Lamormaini," *Archiv für österreichische Geschichte,* 54, pt. 2 (1876): 282.

53. Prince Maximilian William to Electress Sophia, 29 December 1699, in Wendland, *Prinzenbriefe,* 45; Declaration of Archduke Leopold to Ferdinand II, 1623, in Renner, "Erbteilung," 220–21.

54. Kunigunde's instructions to her representatives to Maximilian I, May–June? 1514, Krenner, *Landtag 1514,* 456. A typical comment on the worthiness of observing ancestral custom is Duke John William of Saxony-Weimar, 1573, HHStA, Reichskanzlei, *Kleinere Reichsstände, Sachsen-Gotha,* fasc. 441, no fol. no. See also Krause, *Urkunden,* 3:165–66.

55. Isenburg, *Stammtafeln* 1:tables 46–53.

56. Moser, *Staatsrecht* 14:431.

57. Cited in Ludolf, *De introductione,* appendix, fasc. 1, p. 89.

58. For example, Joan Thirsk, "The European Debate on Customs of Inheritance," in Goody et al., *Family and Inheritance,* 189–90.

59. Rommel, *Geschichte* 4:76.

60. Philippe Aries, *Centuries of Childhood: A Social History of Family Life,* trans. Robert Baldick (New York: Vintage, 1962), 371–72.

61. On the Protestant tendency to harmonize civil legal relationships with gospel and divine law, see Guido Kisch, *Melanchthons Rechts- und Soziallehre* (Berlin: de Gruyter, 1967), esp. 80–101. See also Strauss, *Law,* 198–99.

62. Prince Frederick August's Justification to his Father, 1690, in Wendland, *Prinzenbriefe,* 33.

63. Otto Schreiber, *Das Testament des Fürsten Wolfgang von Anhalt (vom 25 August 1565),* Deutschrechtliche Beiträge vol. 9, no. 2 (Heidelberg: Carl Winter, 1913), 62–63.

64. Fritz Hartung, "Der deutsche Fürstenstaat des 16. u. 17. Jahrhunderts nach den fürstlichen Testamenten," in his *Volk und Staat* (Leipzig: Koehler and Amelang, 1940), 97–99.

65. Ludolf, *De introductione,* appendix, fasc. 3, p. 72.

66. HHStA, Familienarchiv, *Familienakten* I.1, *Hausgesetze,* Karton 1, Konv. 1, "Suasio . . . ," fol. 15.

67. *Saalfeldisches Recess-Buch,* 1.

68. Gerald Strauss, *Luther's House of Learning: Indoctrination of the Young in the German Reformation* (Baltimore: John Hopkins University Press, 1978), 144.

69. August Kluckhohn, ed., *Das Testament Friedrichs des Frommen Churfürsten von der Pfalz*, Abhandlungen der historischen Classe der königlich bayerischen Akademie der Wissenschaften, no. 12, pt. 3 (1874): 88.

70. Moser, *Staatsrecht* 13:44; Martin Luther, "Vorrede auff das Buch Jesu Syrach," in *Die gantze Heilige Schrifft Deudsch,* 2 vols. (1545; reprint, Darmstadt: Wissenschaftliche Buchgesellschaft, 1972), 2:1,751; Schulze, *Erstgeburt,* 337. The verse itself is Ecclesiasticus 33:24.

71. Johann Christian Lünig, *Das Teutsche Reichs-Archiv,* 24 folio vols. (Leipzig: Lanck, 1710–22), vol. 5, pt. 2:95–96; Renner, "Erbteilung," 215.

72. Krause, *Urkunden* 1:729–30.

73. Moser, *Staatsrecht* 12:474; Schulze, *Hausgesetze* 3:107.

74. Krause, *Urkunden* 3:141–44.

75. Gelbke, *Ernst der Fromme* 1:43; Georg Mentz, *Weimarische Staats- und Regentengeschichte vom westfälischen Frieden bis zum Regierungsantritt Carl Augusts,* part 1 of *Carl August. Darstellungen und Briefe zur Geschichte des weimarischen Fürstenhauses und Landes* (Jena: Bidermann, 1936), 48. On the merits of the *Seniorat* see the memorandum of the imperial judicial hearing on the Hesse-Kassel dispute ca. 1650–52, HHStA, Reichskanzlei, *Kleinere Reichsstände, Hessen-Cassel,* fasc. 156, fols. 469, 479.

76. Anonymous memorandum on the primogeniture conflict in HHStA, Reichskanzlei, *Kleinere Reichsstände, Hessen-Cassel,* fasc. 155, Konv. "De anno 1636," no fol. no.; and memorandum of the Aulic Council (sketch), ca. 1650–52, ibid., fasc. 156, fol. 458.

77. Elector Frederick III of the Palatine's description of the Saxon territorial division of 1566, HHStA, Reichskanzlei, *Kleinere Reichsstände, Sachsen-Gotha,* fasc. 439, no fol. no.; Duke George of Saxony-Gotha's primogeniture order of 1680 in Moser, *Staatsrecht* 12:489; *Recess-Buch,* 51, 56.

78. Schulze, *Hausgesetze* 1:31. The text of the prayer is in Johann Christoph Beckmann, *Historia des Furstentums [sic] Anhalt,* 3 vols. (Zerbst: Zimmerman, 1710–16), 2:178.

79. Lünig, *Reichs-Archiv,* vol. 5, pt. 2:140–41.

80. Schulze, *Hausgesetze* 3:74; August of Anhalt-Zerbst to his chancellor and councillors, 22 May 1636, in Krause, *Urkunden,* 3:162.

81. Gelbke, *Ernst der Fromme* 3:33.

82. Beckmann, *Historia* 1:74, 76.

83. Thirsk, in Goody et al., "Inheritance," 188–89; Schulze, *Hausgesetze* 1:31; *Recess-Buch,* 65, 68.

84. *Recess-Buch,* 76.

85. Moser, *Staatsrecht* 12:464. Cf. Schulze, *Erstgeburt,* 340.

86. Kunst, *Evangelischer Glaube,* 14; Gerhard Müller, "Luther und die evangelischen Fürsten," 65–83, and Volker Press, "Sozialen Kräfte," 193–96, in *Luther,* ed. Iserloh and Müller.

87. Martin Luther to Elector John Frederick and Duke Maurice of Saxony, 7 April 1542, D. *Martin Luthers Werke, Briefwechsel,* 18 vols. (Weimar: Böhlaus,, 1930–85), 10:31, 34–35. See also Luther to Princess Margaret of Anhalt, 22 November 1543, ibid., p. 447, and to Counts Albert, Philip, and John George of Mansfeld, 15 June 1542, ibid., pp. 82–83.

88. Martin Luther to Count Albert of Mansfeld, 1525, in Luther, *Briefwechsel* 3:414, 416.

89. Lünig, *Reichs-Archiv,* vol. 5, pt. 2:95–96. Cf. Schulze, *Erstgeburt,* 340.

90. Cited in Schulze, *Erstgeburt,* 408.

91. Andreas Räss, *Die Convertiten seit der Reformation,* 14 vols. (Freiburg im Breisgau: Herder, 1866–80), 5:468, 484–88, 490.

Chapter II: "Gott macht Kinder"

1. Luther, "Vom ehelichen Leben" (1522), *Werke,* 10:304.

2. Leopold I to Graf Pötting, 3 July 1665, in *Privatbriefe Kaiser Leopold I an den Grafen F. E. Pötting 1662–73,* ed. Alfred Pribram and Moriz Landwehr von Pragenau, Fontes Rerum Austriacarum, Diplomataria et Acta (Vienna: Gerold, 1903), 56:13; Leopold to Pötting, 9 February 1664, 42–43 and *n*3.

3. Aloys Schulte, *Der Adel und die deutsche Kirche im Mittelalter* (Stuttgart: Enke, 1910), 258.

4. Declaration of Ferdinand II to Archduke Leopold, 1623, in Renner, "Erbteilung," 219.

5. Maximilian's Instructions to his representatives, 20 December 1513, in Krenner, *Landtag 1514,* 31–32.

6. William Walker Rockwell, *Die Doppelehe des Landgrafen Philipp von Hessen* (Marburg: Elwert, 1904), 65–66; William of Hesse-Kassel's Instructions to Simon Bing, 1566, in Rommel, *Geschichte,* 4:447.

7. Schulze, *Erstgeburt,* 341–42; Johann Gustav Droysen, ed., "Das Testament des grossen Kurfürsten," *Abhandlungen der philologisch-historischen Klasse der königlichen sächsischen Gesellschaft der Wissenschaften,* 5 (1870): 98, 101. See also Landgrave William of Hesse to Count Palatine Ludwig, 28 December 1571, *Briefe Friedrich des Frommen,* vol. 2, pt. 1:440.

8. For example, Marburg SA, Bestand 4f: Staatenabteilung, *Sachsen-Weissenfels,* nos. 2–8.

9. Count Günther of Waldeck to William IV of Hesse-Kassel, Marburg SA, Bestand 4f: Staatenabteilung, *Waldeck,* no. 95.

10. Vienna, HHStA, Familienarchiv, *Familienakten II.1, Entbindungen und Taufen,* Karton 18, Konv. II.1, fol. 48.

11. Ibid., fols. 22, 26–27, 31–36.

12. All calculations done from tables in vol. 1 of Isenburg, *Stammtafeln.*

13. Sigismund Peller, "Births and Deaths among Europe's Ruling Families," in *Population in History,* ed. David Glass and D. E. C. Eversley (London: Arnold, 1965), 98, table 10.

14. Peller, "Mortality," pt. 1, 429; Richard Koebner, "Die Eheauffassung des ausgehenden Mittelalters," *Archiv für Kulturgeschichte,* 9 (1911–12), 139.

15. Strauss, *Luther's House,* 89, 332 n3; Thomas McKeown, *The Modern Rise of Population* (London: Arnold, 1976), 24; Pierre Chaunu, *La Civilisation de l'Europe classique* (Paris: Arthaud, 1966), 190–91. On Maximilian II see Lucian Grauer to Hanns Lamberg, Vienna, HHStA, Familienarchiv, *Familienakten* II.1, *Entbindungen und Taufen,* Karton 19, Konv. I, fol. 19 (undated). For Maximilian I of Bavaria see William V of Bavaria to Albert V of Bavaria in Hubert Glaser, ed., *Um Glauben und Reich. Kurfürst Maximilian I,* vol. 2, pt. 2 of Wittelsbach und Bayern, 3 vols. in 6 parts (Munich: Hirmer, Piper, 1980), 97. See also Steven Ozment, *When Fathers Ruled: Family Life in Reformation Europe* (Cambridge: Harvard University Press, 1983), 118–19.

16. Frank Lorimer, *Culture and Human Fertility* (Paris: UNESCO, 1954), 81, 202.

17. John T. Noonan, *Contraception: A History of Its Treatment by the Catholic Theologians and Canonists* (Cambridge, Mass.: Belknap, 1965), 312–14, 324; Waldemar Kawerau, *Die Reformation und die Ehe: Ein Beitrag zur Kulturgeschichte des 16. Jahrhunderts,* Schriften des Vereins für Reformationsgeschichte, no. 39 (Halle: Verein für Reformationsgeschichte, 1892), 36(citation)–37.

18. Arnold E. Berger, ed., *Grundzüge evangelischer Lebensformung nach ausgewählten Schriften Martin Luthers* (Leipzig: Reclam, 1930), 199; Christiane Andersson, "Religiöse Bilder Cranachs im Dienste der Reformation," in *Humanismus und Reformation als kulturelle Kräfte in der deutschen Reformation,* ed. Lewis Spitz, Veröffentlichungen der historischen Kommission zu Berlin, no. 51 (Berlin: de Gruyter, 1980), 55; Ozment, *Fathers,* 100.

19. Schulze, *Hausgesetze* 2:227; *Recess-Buch,* 1.

20. Maximilian's Instructions for his ambassadors to Poland, 3,5,10 February 1565, HHStA, Familienarchiv, *Familienakten,* II.5, *Ehescheidungen,* Karton 53, fols. 55, 85–86; Ozment, *Fathers,* 55; Karl Vocelka, *Habsburgische Hochzeiten 1550–1600: Kulturgeschichtliche Studien zum manieristischen Representationsfest,* Veröffentlichungen der Kommission für neuere Geschichte Oesterreichs, no. 65 (Vienna: Böhlaus, 1976), 75; Munich, Hauptstaatsarchiv: Geheimes Haus-Archiv, *Korrespondenz-Akten,* 593/3, no fol. no.

21. See the preliminary draft of Landgrave Maurice's *Ehebrief* of 3 September 1593 in Marburg SA, Bestand 4a, *Landgräfliche Personalien,* Paket 40.3, no fol. no. Also, Rommel, *Geschichte* 4:451; Elisabeth of Saxony-Gotha's letter to Maximilian II is from 5 June 1567 and found in Munich, Bayerisches Hauptstaatsarchiv, Kurbayern, *Aeusseres Archiv,* no. 4302, fol. 222.

22. Philip of Hesse to Henry the Younger of Braunschweig-Wolffenbüttel, *Urkundliche Quellen zur hessischen Reformationsgeschichte.* 4 vols. Veröffentlichungen der historischen Kommission für Hessen und Waldeck 11 (Marburg: Elwert, 1915–55), 2:261–62.

23. Glaser, *Um Glauben und Reich,* vol. 2, pt. 2:297–98; Werner Elert, *Morphologie des Luthertums,* 2 vols. (Munich: Beck, 1931– 32), 2:106; Schulze, *Erstgeburt,* 330.

24. Ludolf, *De introductione,* appendix, fasc. 4, p. 119.

25. Rommel, *Geschichte* 4:318.

26. *Mémoires: Memoiren der Herzogin Sophie nachmals Kurfürstin von Hannover,* ed. Adolf Köcher, Publikationen aus den königlichen preussischen Staatsarchiven, no. 4 (Leipzig: Hirzel, 1879), 76–77.

27. N.n. Ribbeck, "Landgraf Wilhelm IV. von Hessen auf der Brautsuche," *Zeitschrift des Vereins für hessische Geschichte und Landeskunde,* n.s., 23 (1898): 181–82, 187.

28. Henry Julius von Braunschweig-Wolfenbüttel, "Von der Susanna, wie dieselbe fälschlich von zweyen Alten des Ehebruchs beklaget, auch unschuldig verurtheilet, aber entlich durch Schickung Gottes des Allmechtigen vom Daniele errettet, und die Beiden Alten zum Tode verdammet worden." *Bibliothek des litterarischen Vereins in Stuttgart,* no. 36 (Tübingen: Litterarischer Verein, 1855), 63–64, 13–14, 3–4, 29, 170, 208.

29. Rockwell, *Doppelehe,* 3; Walter Sohm, *Territorium und Reformation in der hessischen Geschichte 1526–1555,* Veröffentlichungen der historischen Kommission für Hessen und Waldeck, no. 11, pt. 1 (Marburg: Elwert, 1915), 172–73.

30. Rockwell, *Doppelehe,* 22; Philip of Hesse's declaration to Martin Bucer, November 1539, in *Briefwechsel Landgraf Philipp's des Grossmüthigen von Hessen mit Bucer,* ed. Max Lenz, Publikationen aus den königlichen preussischen Staatsarchiven (Leipzig: Hirzel, 1880–91), 5:353.

31. Philip of Hesse to Luther, 20 June 1540, in Lenz, *Briefwechsel,* 365; Philip of Hesse to Luther, 18 July 1540, ibid., 383.

32. Peter Laslett, "Illegitimate Fertility and the Matrimonial Market," in *Marriage and Remarriage in Populations of the Past,* ed. J. Dupâquier et al. (London: Academic Press, 1981), p. 464.

33. Jean-Louis Flandrin, *Families in Former Times: Kinship, Household, and Sexuality.* (Cambridge: Cambridge University Press, 1979), 196–98; J. Houdaille, "Fécondité des familles souveraines du XVIe au XVIIIe siècle: influence de l'âge du père sur la fécondité," *Population* 31 (1976): 956; Chaunu, *Europe classique,* 196–97; Étienne Hélin, *La démographie de Liège aux XVIIe et XVIIIe siècles,* Académie royale de Belgique, Classe des lettres. Mémoires 56, no. 4 (Brussels: Palais des Académies, 1963), 210; Laurence Stone, "The New Eighteenth Century," *The New York Review of Books* 31, no. 5 (March 1984), 46. Even those most inclined to discount the impact of

religion on population patterns—for example, Edward Shorter, "Illegitimacy, Sexual Revolution, and Social Change in Modern Europe," in *Marriage and Fertility: Studies in Interdisciplinary History,* ed. Robert I. Rotberg and Theodore K. Rabb (Princeton: Princeton University Press, 1980), 108—admit that moral values have some bearing on coital practice. See Shorter's "Sexual Change and Illegitimacy: The European Experience," in *Modern European Social History,* ed. Robert Bezucha (Lexington, Mass.: Heath, 1972), 234.

34. Noonan, *Contraception,* 312–14.

35. Strauss, *House of Learning,* 110, 112.

36. Koebner, "Eheauffassung," 151, 198 *n*1.

37. Jacques Solé, *L'amour en occident à l'époque moderne* (Paris: Michel, 1976), 78; Jean-Louis Flandrin, "Contraception, mariage, et relations amoureuses dans l'occident chrétien," *Annales ESC* (1969): 1380–81; Strauss, *House of Learning,* 110–11; Kawerau, *Ehe,* 16; Lyndal Roper, "Luther: Sex, Marriage, and Motherhood," *History Today* 33 (December 1983): 35.

38. A. Bideau and A. Perrenoud, "Remariage et fécondité: Contribution à l'étude des mécanismes de récuperation des populations anciennes," in *Marriage and Remarriage,* ed. Dupâquier et al., 557; Ruth Kleinman, *Anne of Austria: Queen of France* (Columbus, Ohio: Ohio State University Press, 1985), 86–87.

39. Eduard Vehse, *Geschichte der deutschen Höfe seit der Reformation,* 48 vols. (Hamburg: Hoffmann und Campe, 1851–60), 30:44 and 31:147–48, 167; Ragnhild Hatton, *George I: Elector and King* (Cambridge: Harvard University Press, 1978), 23 and table 1.

40. "Septem Questiones Principales ex statu Causa Hesso Casellona et circumstantiis eiusdem resultantes. Centum Regalis seu canonibus definitae," Vienna, HHStA, Reichskanzlei, *Kleinere Reichsstände, Hessen-Cassel,* fasc. 156, fols. 189–90.

41. Lazareth, *Christian Home,* 229; Elert, *Morphologie* 2:103; Lünig, *Reichs-Archiv,* vol. 5, pt. 2:172.

42. Franz Dominicus Häberlin, *Neueste teutsche Reichsgeschichte vom Anfange des Schmalkaldischen Krieges bis auf unsere Zeiten,* 20 vols. (Halle: Gebauer, 1774–86), 14:438.

43. Elector Frederick III of the Palatine's description of Saxon agreement, Vienna, HHStA, Reichskanzlei, *Kleinere Reichsstände, Sachsen-Gotha,* fasc. 439, no fol. no.

44. Codicil to Landgrave Maurice's testament (copy), Vienna, HHStA, Reichskanzlei, *Kleinere Reichsstände, Hessen-Cassel,* fasc. 153, no fol. no. See also Philip of Hesse's Declaration to Christine of Saxony, 11 December 1539, in Lenz, *Briefwechsel,* vol. 5, pt. 1:359.

45. Seckendorff, *Fürstenstaat,* 160.

46. Ibid.

47. Lünig, *Reichs-Archiv*, vol. 5, pt. 2:298.

48. Rommel, *Geschichte* 6:315 *n*29.

49. Schulze, *Hausgesetze* 2:278.

50. Maximilian II to Albert V of Bavaria, 18 October 1566, in *Die Korrespondenz Maximilians II*, ed. Viktor Bibl. Veröffentlichungen der Kommission für neuere Geschichte Oesterreichs, vols. 14, 16 (Vienna: Holzhausen, 1916–21), 14:37.

51. Anonymous memorandum entitled "Bedenckhen vnnd Vrsachen warumb ain Regierender Herzog in Bayrn es mit vermehrung der Deputat weiter nit als der Vätterlich Testament vermag beisprungen khind oder soll," 1610?, Munich, Hauptstaatsarchiv, Geheimes Haus-Archiv, *Korrespondenz-Akten*, no. 945, no fol. no.; Maximilian I of Bavaria to the Elector of Cologne, 11 April 1611, ibid., no fol. no.; Sigmund Riezler, *Geschichte Baierns*, 8 vols. (Gotha: Perthes, 1878–1914), 4:648.

52. Anton Karl Mally, *Der österreichische Kreis in der Executionsordnung des römisch-deutschen Reiches*, Wiener Dissertationen aus dem Gebiete der Geschichte, no. 8 (Vienna: Geyer, 1967), 42–43; Domke, *Viril-Stimmen*, 127–28.

53. Stürmberger, "Anfänge," 42–43.

54. Archdukes Albert and Maximilian to Emperor Matthias, 13 December 1615, Vienna, HHStA, Familienarchiv, *Familienakten* I.1, *Hausgesetze*, Karton 3, fol. 8; Archduke Ferdinand to Emperor Matthias, 9 September 1616, ibid., fol. 141. The general air of high seriousness comes through most clearly in the correspondence of Archdukes Albert and Maximilian, 1615–16, in ibid., bundle "Matthias, Albrecht, Maximilian," fols. 1–104.

Philip III of Spain ceded his claims to Hungary and Bohemia to Ferdinand on the condition that if the latter had no male heir, these lands would revert to the Spanish line and its offspring. See Johann Franzl, *Ferdinand II: Kaiser im Zwiespalt der Zeit* (Graz: Styria, 1978), 152–58.

55. "Bedenckhen," Munich, Hauptstaatsarchiv, Geheimes Haus-Archiv, *Korrespondenz-Akten*, no. 945, no fol. no. On taxation in Bavaria see Heinz Dollinger, *Studien zur Finanzreform Maximilians I. von Bayern in den Jahren 1598–1618*, Schriftenreihe der historischen Kommission bei der bayerischen Akademie der Wissenschaften, no. 8 (Göttingen: Vandenhoek und Ruprecht, 1968), chaps. 2 and 3.

56. "Bedenckhen," Munich, Geheimes Haus-Archiv, *Korrespondenz-Akten*, no. 945, no fol. no.

57. Heinz Dollinger, "Kurfürst Maximilian I. von Bayern und Justus Lipsius, *Archiv für Kulturgeschichte* 46 (1964): 227–80; Oestreich, *Neostoicism*, 98–100; Robert Bireley, *Maximilian von Bayern, Adam Contzen, S.J., und die Gegenreformation in Deutschland 1624–1635*, Schriftenreihe der historischen

Kommission bei der bayerischen Akademie der Wissenschaften, no. 13 (Göttingen: Vandenhoek und Ruprecht, 1975), 15, 18.

58. Ficker, *Reichsfuerstenstände*, 265; "Bedenckhen," Munich, Geheimes Haus-Archiv, *Korrespondenz-Akten*, no. 945, no fol. no.

59. Schulze, *Erstgeburt*, 372–80.

60. William V of Bavaria to Bavarian ducal councillors in Felix Stieve, ed., *Briefe und Akten zur Geschichte des dreissigjährigen Krieges*, vols. 4 and 5 of Abhandlungen der historischen Kommission der königlichen bayerischen Akademie der Wissenschaften (Munich: Rieger, 1878–95), 4:528; Dollinger, *Finanzreform*, 29.

61. Munich, Hauptstaatsarchiv, Geheimes Haus-Archiv, *Korrespondenz-Akten*, no. 932, no fol. no.

62. Maximilian's resolution of 1611?, Munich, Geheimes Haus-Archiv, *Korrespondenz-Akten*, no. 945, no fol. no. See also ibid., no. 929, no fol. no.; and Dollinger, *Finanzreform*, 49.

63. Stürmberger, "Anfänge," 153.

64. Duke Ernest of Bavaria to Dr. Andrae [Andreas Fabrizius], September–October 1570?, Munich, Hauptstaatsarchiv, *Kasten Schwarz*, no. 865, fol. 78.

65. Manfred Weitlauff, "Die Reichskirchenpolitik des Hauses Bayern im Zeichen gegenreformatorischen Engagements und österreich-bayerischen Gegensatzes," in Glaser, *Um Glauben*, vol. 2, pt. 1:50.

66. Hanns Müller to Archduke Leopold, 13 December 1607, Vienna, HHStA, Familienarchiv, *Familienakten* VIII, *Varia,* Karton 109, no fol. no. Müller was the archduke's confidential secretary.

67. Ibid.

68. Felix Strauss, "Herzog Ernst von Bayern (1500–1560)," *Mitteilungen der Gesellschaft für Salzburger Landeskunde* 101 (1969): 270.

69. William V of Bavaria to the Archbishop of Salzburg, 26 April 1601, Stieve, *Dreissigjähriger Krieg* 4:496–97.

70. Weitlauff, "Reichskirchenpolitik," 53.

71. Karl August Muffat, "Die Ansprüche des Herzogs Ernst, Administrators des Hochstiftes Passau, auf einen dritten Teil und an die Mitregierung des Herzogthumes Bayern," *Bayerische Akademie der Wissenschaften: Abhandlungen der philosophisch-historischen Klasse*, no. 38 (1867): 116–17; Schulte, *Adel und Kirche*, 282; Dudik, "Korrespondenz," 222.

72. Günther von Lojewski, *Bayerns Weg nach Köln: Geschichte der bayerischen Bistumspolitik in der 2. Hälfte des 16. Jahrhunderts*, Bonner historische Forschungen, no. 21 (Bonn: Röhrscheid, 1962), 16–18; Günther von Lojewski, "Bayerns Kampf um Köln," in Glaser, *Um Glauben*, vol. 2, pt. 1:44–45; Hans Feine, *Die Besetzung der Reichsbistümer vom westfälischen Frieden bis zur Säkularisation 1648–1803*, Kirchenrechtliche Abhandlungen, no. 97/98 (Stuttgart: Enke, 1921), 316; Wilhelm Dersch,

"Beiträge zur Geschichte des Kardinals Friedrich von Hessen," *Zeitschrift des Vereins für Geschichte und Altertum Schlesiens* 62 (1928): 272, 279.

73. [Franz] Burckhardt to Albert V of Bavaria, 7 May 1575, Munich, Hauptstaatsarchiv, *Kasten Schwarz,* no. 866, fol. 22; Albrecht of Bavaria to Dr. [Hermann] Winckler, 23 February 1575, ibid., fol. 3; Andreas Fabrizius to Duke William V, 14 December 1577, ibid., no. 7395, fols. 74–75; Archduke Ferdinand to Archduke Maximilian, 4 April 1607, Vienna, HHStA, Familienarchiv, *Familienakten* VIII, *Varia,* Karton 109, no fol. no.; Emperor Rudolph to Archduke Maximilian, 9 December 1607, ibid., no fol. no.; Lojewski, "Kampf," 45.

74. Archduke Leopold to the Archbishop of Mainz, 4 December 1607, HHStA, Familienarchiv, *Familienakten* VIII, *Varia,* Karton 109, no fol. no.

75. Ernest of Bavaria to Dr. Andrae, September–October 1570?, Munich, Hauptstaatsarchiv, *Kasten Schwarz,* no. 865, fol. 78.

76. Karl Otmar Freiherr von Aretin, *Heiliges Römisches Reich 1776–1806: Reichsverfassung und Staatssouveränität,* 2 vols. (Wiesbaden: Steiner, 1967), 2:25–26.

77. See especially Vienna, HHStA, Familienarchiv, *Familienakten* I.1, *Hausgesetze,* Karton 3. See also Lojewski, "Kampf," 43 and passim.

78. "Suasio," HHStA, Familienarchiv, *Familienakten* I.1, *Hausgesetze,* Karton 1, fol. 14.

79. Heinemann, *Geschichte von Braunschweig* 2:335; Dersch, "Beiträge," 272; Weitlauff, "Reichskirchenpolitik," 51.

80. Isenburg, *Stammtafeln,* vol. 4: tables 118, 127–29; and vol. 5: tables 151–55.

81. Robert Bireley, S.J., *Religion and Politics in the Age of the Counterreformation. Emperor Ferdinand II, William Lamoramaini, S.J., and the Formation of Imperial Policy* (Chapel Hill, N. C.: University of North Carolina Press, 1981), 26; Feine, *Besetzung,* 50–53, 306.

82. Schulze, *Hausgesetze* 2:55.

83. Landgrave William IV to Ludwig, Count Palatine, 28 December 1571, in Kluckhohn, *Briefe Friedrich des Frommen,* vol. 2, pt. 1:440.

84. Ludolf, *De introductione,* appendix, fasc. 3, pp. 40–44.

85. Ibid., fasc, 4, pp. 107–08.

86. Schnath, *Geschichte Hannovers* 1:277–78.

Chapter III: Changing Values, Changing Times

1. Heinemann, *Geschichte von Braunschweig* 2:280–81; Karl Freiherr von Bothmer and Georg Schnath, eds., *Aus den Erinnerungen des Hans Kaspar von Bothmer,* Quellen und Darstellungen zur Geschichte Niedersachsens, vol. 44 (Hildesheim: Lax, 1936), 63.

2. Walter Junge, *Leibniz und der sachsen-lauenburgische Erbfolgestreit,* Quellen

und Darstellungen zur Geschichte Niedersachsens, vol. 65 (Hildesheim: Lax, 1965), passim.

3. Fritz Dickmann, *Der westfälische Frieden* (Münster: Aschendorff, 1959), 29–30, 32; Jean Baptiste Neveux, *Vie spirituelle et vie sociale entre Rhin et Baltique au 17e siècle* (Paris: Klincksieck, 1967), 306; Rosemarie Aulinger, *Das Bild des Reichstages im 16. Jahrhundert: Beiträge zu einer typologischen Analyse schriftlicher und bildlicher Quellen,* Schriftenreihe der historischen Kommission bei der bayerischen Akademie der Wissenschaften, no. 18 (Göttingen: Vandenhoek und Ruprecht, 1980), 242–43.

4. Vienna, HHStA, Reichskanzlei, *Kleinere Reichsstände, Hessen-Cassel,* fasc. 153, pt. 2, p. 79; ibid., fasc. 157, no fol. no.; Volker Press, *Calvinismus und Territorialstaat: Regierung und Zentralbehörden der Kurpfalz 1559–1619,* Kieler historische Studien, no. 7 (Stuttgart: Klett, 1970), 269–70.

5. John William of Saxony to Emperor Maximilian II, 10 December 1572, Vienna, HHStA, Reichskanzlei, *Kleinere Reichsstände, Sachsen-Gotha,* fasc. 440, no fol. no.; Elector August of Saxony to the Weimar councillors, 1573?, ibid., fasc. 441, no fol. no.

6. Heinemann, *Geschichte von Braunschweig* 2:352–53.

7. Max Spindler, *Handbuch der bayerischen Geschichte,* 2d ed., 4 vols. (Munich: Beck, 1977–81), 2:163, 195–96.

8. Kurt Dülfer, "Fürst und Verwaltung: Grundzüge der hessischen Verwaltungsgeschichte im 16.–19. Jahrhundert," *Hessisches Jahrbuch für Landesgeschichte* 3 (1953): 153; Ernest of Hesse-Rheinfels-Rotenburg, "Das Schicksal der Kinder Philipps des Grossmütigen aus seiner Ehe mit Margarethe von der Saal," *Historische-politische Blätter für das katholische Deutschland* 20 (1847): 94; Rockwell, *Doppelehe,* 35; Dickmann, *Westfälische Frieden,* 29; Francis L. Carsten, *Princes and Parliaments in Germany from the Fifteenth to the Eighteenth Century* (Oxford: Clarendon, 1959), 170, 172.

9. Schulze, *Erstgeburt,* 311; Karl Bosl, *Bayerische Geschichte* (Munich: List, 1971), 114–15, 118; Karl Bosl, *Die Geschichte der Repräsentation in Bayern* (Munich: Beck, 1974), 125–26.

10. Jürgen Freiherr von Kruedener, *Die Rolle des Hofes im Absolutismus,* Forschungen zur Sozial- und Wirtschaftsgeschichte, no. 19 (Stuttgart: Fischer, 1973), 13–17.

11. Rommel, *Geschichte* 5:76 n16; Kurt Hermann, *Die Erbteilungen im Hause Schwarzburg* (Halle: John, 1919), 76–77.

12. Rommel, *Geschichte* 5:76 n16; Vienna, HHStA, Familienarchiv, *Familienakten* I.1, *Hausgesetze,* Karton 3, bundle "Gutachten der drey kaiserlichen Brüder . . . ," fols. 32–33; Elector Frederick III of the Palatine's report on the Saxon division, ibid., Reichskanzlei, *Kleinere Reichsstände, Sachsen-Gotha,* fasc. 439, no fol. no. Elector Frederick conducted the negotiations

and, along with Saxon dukes, signed the agreement. Also John William's memorandum to Maximilian II, 10 March 1566, ibid., *Sachsen-Weimar,* fasc. 449, fol. 2.

13. Karl E. Demandt, "Amt und Familie," *Hessisches Jahrbuch für Landes-geschichte* 2 (1952): 91, 119; William IV of Hesse to Landgrave Philip of Hesse-Rheinfels, 4 March 1571, Rommel, *Geschichte* 5:740–45; Ludwig Zimmermann, *Der ökonomische Staat Landgraf Wilhelms IV,* 2 vols., Veröffentlichungen der historischen Kommission für Hessen und Waldeck, no. 17, pts. 1 and 2 (Marburg: Elwert, 1933–34), 1:150.

14. Moser, *Teutsches Staatsrecht* 12:467.

15. Schulze, *Hausgesetze* 2:103–04.

16. Horst Kraemer, *Der deutsche Kleinstaat des 17. Jahrhunderts im Spiegel von Seckendorffs "Teutschen Furstenstaat"* (1922–24; reprint, Darmstadt: Wissenschaftliche Buchgesellschaft, 1974), 27–28. On the Habsburg problems see Innsbruck, Tiroler Landesarchiv, *Geschäft von Hof,* 1568–1574, 1576, passim.

17. Vienna, HHStA, Reichskanzlei, *Kleinere Reichsstände, Hessen-Cassel,* fasc. 153, "Bericht," fol. 4.

18. The map, with no folio number, is in Marburg SA, Bestand 4f: Staatenabteilung: *Sachsen-Weimar,* Paket 24.

19. For a representative sample see Ludolf, *De introductione,* appendix, fasc. 8, pp. 3–61.

20. Cited in Schulze, *Erstgeburt,* 36, ". . . allein der zanksüchtigen Welt Spaltungen und Irrungen halber. . . ."

21. Report of imperial commissioners, 2 July 1572, Vienna, HHStA, Reichskanzlei, *Kleinere Reichsstände, Sachsen-Gotha,* fasc. 440, no fol. no.

22. Vienna, HHStA, Reichskanzlei, *Kleinere Reichsstände, Hessen-Cassel,* fasc. 156, fols. 89–93, 594.

23. Dorothy Susanna to Emperor Maximilian II, 12 May 1573 (copy), Vienna, HHStA, Reichskanzlei, *Kleinere Reichsstände, Sachsen-Gotha,* fasc. 441, no fol. no.

24. Demandt, "Amt," 107–09, 111.

25. Mack Walker, *Johann Jakob Moser and the Holy Roman Empire of the German Nation* (Chapel Hill, N. C.: University of North Carolina Press, 1981), 174; Krause, *Urkunden* 3:144; Pischel, "Zentralverwaltung" 20:265.

26. Reports of the imperial commission, 10 December 1572, Vienna, HHStA, Reichskanzlei, *Kleinere Reichsstände, Sachsen-Gotha,* fasc. 441, no fol. no.; John William of Saxony to Maximilian II, 10 December 1572, ibid., no fol. no.; report of imperial commission, 1572 (no further date), ibid., no fol. no.; "Sächsischer Vormunder . . . ," 8 February 1573, ibid., no fol. no.; "Bericht . . . ," ibid., *Hessen-Cassel,* Karton 153, fols. 196–97.

27. Johann Gottlob Immanuel Breitkopf, "Ueber Buchdruckerey und Buch-

handlung in Leipzig," *Journal für Fabrik, Manufaktur, Handlung, und Mode* 4 (July 1793): 2–4. Professor Egbert Krispyn of the department of German at the University of Georgia in Athens kindly brought this item to my attention.

28. ". . . nimands kan zweien widerwartigen herrn, zugleich dienen unnd dieselben pro patronis agnoscirn unnd venerirn, sonderlich in Religion sachen." Vienna, HHStA, Reichskanzlei, *Kleinere Reichsstände, Sachsen-Gotha,* fasc. 440, no fol. no.

29. Moser, *Staatsrecht* 14:159–70.

30. The clergy of Neustadt to the Council of Schaffhausen, December 1577, in Friedrich Bezold, ed., *Briefe des Pfalzgrafen Johann Kasimir mit verwandten Schriftstücken,* 3 vols. (Munich: Rieger, 1882–1903), 1:289.

31. ". . . dass man in diesen Landen allezeit etwas zu reformiren haben müssen. . . ," Krause, *Urkunden* 3:158; see also 868*n* and 872.

32. Duke John William's "Gravamina", 26 May 1571, Vienna, HHStA, Reichsarchiv, *Kleinere Reichsstände, Sachsen-Gotha,* fasc. 439, no fol. no.

33. Maximilian's Instructions to the second Bavarian diet in 1514 in Krenner, *Landtag 1514,* 305; J. G. von Koeppler, *Die Wirklichkeit der Domainien in Baiern* (Munich: Churfürstliche akademische Buchdruckerey, 1768), appendix, 60–61.

34. "In puncto juris primogenituris," excerpted and summarized in Häberlin, *Reichsgeschichte* 14:442–43.

35. Ernest von Hesse-Rheinfels-Rotenburg, "Schicksal," 94.

36. Zimmermann, *Ökonomischer Staat* 1:16.

37. Ludwig, Count Palatine to Landgrave William of Hesse, 12 October 1569, Kluckhohn, *Briefe Friedrich des Frommen,* vol. 2, pt. 1:364.

38. Moser, *Staatsrecht* 14:159–70. Cf. Schulze, *Erstgeburt,* 375–76.

39. Ludolf, *De introductione,* appendix, fasc. 3, p. 101.

40. Schulze, *Erstgeburt,* 344, 347–52, 410, 425, 427, 440–44, 446–47.

41. Carsten, *Princes and Parliaments,* 175–80; Geoffrey Parker, *The Thirty Years' War* (London: Routledge and Kegan Paul, 1984), 224.

42. Princes John Casimir and George Aribert of Anhalt to Prince Ludwig, 31 August 1637, Krause, *Urkunden,* vol. 4, pt. 1:249–50. Cf. Prince August of Anhalt-Zerbst to Princes Ludwig, John Casimir, and George Aribert, 26 August 1637, p. 244.

43. Ibid., pt. 1:iv.

44. Ludolf, *De introductione,* appendix, fasc. 2, pp. 28–29. For the especially heavy impact of the French and Turkish conflicts on smaller principalities see the Counts of Schwarzburg to Emperor Leopold I, 18 March 1682, HHStA, *Kleinere Reichsstände, Schwarzburg,* fasc. 500, no fol. no. and the Counts of Reuss-Plauen to Leopold I, 20 December 1690, ibid., *Reuss-Plauen,* fasc. 423, no fol. no.

45. Oestreich, *Neostoicism,* 215.

46. Otto Schaer, *Der Staatshaushalt des Kurfürstentums Hannover unter dem Kurfürsten Ernst August 1680–1698,* Forschungen zur Geschichte Niedersachsens, no. 4 (Hannover: Geibel, 1912), 36, 39–40, 49, 55, 60.

47. Ibid., 39–40; Gerhard Schilfert, *Deutschland von 1648 bis 1789* (Berlin: Deutscher Verlag der Wissenschaften, 1962), 559–61, 63.

48. Wilhelm Lüdtke, "Veit Ludwig von Seckendorf als deutscher Staatsmann und Volkserzieher des 17. Jahrhunderts," *Jahrbuch der Akademie zu Erfurt,* n.s., 54 (1939): 55; Lehmann, *Absolutismus,* 18.

49. Ludolf, *De introductione,* appendix, fasc. 2, pp. 28–29.

50. Dietrich, *Testamente,* 88.

51. Rabb, *Struggle,* 80, 117; Parker, *Thirty Years' War,* 219; Karl Holl, *Die Bedeutung der grossen Kriege für das religiöse und kirchliche Leben innerhalb des deutschen Protestantismus* (Tübingen: Mohr, 1917), 22–38. Cf. Lehmann, *Absolutismus,* 16–17.

52. Ludolf, *De introductione,* appendix, fasc. 2, p. 29; fasc. 4, pp. 118–19; fasc. 5, p. 172.

53. Bothmer, *Erinnerungen,* 62–63; Schulze, *Hausgesetze* 2:278.

54. Friedrich August Freiherr o Byrn, "Christian, Herzog zu Sachsen-Weissenfels, kursächsischer General-Feld-Marschall Lieutenant, *Archiv für die sächsische Geschichte,* n.s., 6 (1880): 71.

55. Prince Frederick August to Duchess Sophia, 11 February 1688, in Wendland, *Prinzenbriefe,* 23.

56. Elert, *Morphologie* 2:104–05.

57. Ibid., 105, 109 and *n.*

58. R. J. W. Evans, *The Making of the Habsburg Monarchy, 1550–1700* (Oxford: Clarendon, 1979), 283–84.

59. Christian of Waldeck to Landgrave Karl of Hesse, 3 February 1688, Marburg SA, Bestand 4f, *Waldeck,* no. 342; Ludolf, *De introductione,* appendix, fasc. 5, p. 172.

60. Ludolf, *De introductione,* appendix, fasc. 2, p. 30.

61. Ibid., p. 101.

62. ibid., fasc. 8, p. 24.

63. Ibid., fasc. 2, pp. 30, 99.

64. Moser, *Staatsrecht* 12:496.

65. Duchess Sophia to Prince Frederick August, 1685?, in Wendland, *Prinzenbriefe,* 2; Sophia to Frederick August, 14 January 1685, p.4.

66. Moser, *Staatsrecht* 13:431–32; Schulze, *Erstgeburt,* 355.

67. Frieda Freiin von Esebeck, *Die Begründung der hannoverschen Kurwürde,* Quellen und Darstellungen zur Geschichte Niedersachsens, no. 43 (Hildesheim: Lax, 1935), 2, 6.

68. Schnath, *Geschichte Hannovers* 1:732 and *n*1; Hajo Holborn, *A History of Modern Germany,* 3 vols. (New York: Knopf, 1959–69), 2:40–41.

69. Esebeck, *Begründung,* 2, 6.

70. Neveux, *Vie spirituelle*, 687–89, 688 *n*351.
71. Edmund Pfleiderer, *Gottfried Wilhelm von Leibniz als Patriot, Staatsmann und Bildungsträger* (Leipzig: Fue's Verlag, 1870), 412. For Leibniz's views on confessional reconciliation see Emilienne Naert, *La Pensée politique de Leibniz* (n.p.: Presses Universitaires, 1964), 74–102; and Neveux, *Vie spirituelle*, 691–92.
72. Elert, *Morphologie*, 2:109, 110 *n*1.
73. Vienna, HHStA, Familienarchiv, *Familienakten* I.1, *Hausgesetze*, Karton 3, bundle "Conferenzprotokolle und Originalvertrage an Kaiser Karl VI . . . ," fol. 37.
74. Ernest August's instructions on primogeniture to his councillors Ernest von Platen and Otto Grote, 31 December 1684 and 1 January 1685 in Schnath, *Geschichte Hannovers* 1:736 (see also 739–40).
75. Ibid., 736.
76. Ibid., 280.
77. Oestreich, *Neostoicism*, 98, 100.
78. Ibid., 109.
79. Ludolf, *De introductione*, appendix, fasc. 4, p. 114.
80. For a succinct summary of scholarship on this question see Peter Blickle, *Landschaften im alten Reich* (Munich: Beck, 1973), 30–47. In general, see Carsten, *Princes and Parliaments*.
81. Winfried Schulze, "Gerhard Oestreich's Begriff 'Sozialdisziplinierung' in der frühen Neuzeit," *Zeitschrift für historische Forschung* 14 (1987): 271. On the question of the restrictions on princely whim that absolutism brought with it, see Barbara Stollberg-Rilinger, *Der Staat als Maschine: Zur politischen Metaphorik des absoluten Fürstenstaats*, Historische Forschungen, no. 30 (Berlin: Duncker und Humblot, 1986), 247.

REFERENCES

Archives

Innsbruck. Tiroler Landesarchiv. *Geschäft von Hof:* 1568–74, 1576.
Marburg. Hessisches Staatsarchiv. Bestand 4a: *Politische Akten nach Philipp dem Grossen:* Abteilung a: *Landgräfliche Personalien,* 38.1, 38.2, 38.3, 38.4, 38.5, 40.3. Bestand 4f: Staatenabteilung: *Sachsen-Weimar,* 24; *Sachsen-Weissenfels,* 2–8; *Waldeck,* 95, 342.
Munich. Bayerisches Staatsarchiv. Geheimes Haus-Archiv. *Korrespondenz-Akten:* 593/3, 929, 932, 945. Hauptstaatsarchiv. *Kasten Schwarz:* 865, 866, 7395; Kurbayern: *Äusseres Archiv,* 4302.
Vienna. Haus-, Hof-, und Staatsarchiv. Familienarchiv. *Familienakten:* I.1, *Hausgesetze,* Karton 1, Konv. 1, Karton 3; *Familienakten:* II.1, *Entbindungen und Taufen,* Karton 18; II.5, *Ehescheidungen,* Karton 53; II.8, *Testamente und Verlassenschaften,* Karton 70; VIII, *Varia,* Karton 109; Reichskanzlei, *Kleinere Reichsstände, Hessen-Cassel,* fascs. 153, 155, 156, 157; *Reuss-Plauen,* fasc. 423; *Schwarzburg,* fasc 500; *Sachsen-Gotha,* fascs. 439, 440, 441; *Sachsen-Weimar,* fasc. 449.

Published Sources

Bezold, Friedrich von, ed. *Briefe des Pfalzgrafen Johann Kasimir mit verwandten Schriftstücken.* 3 vols. Munich: Rieger, 1882–1903.
Bibl, Viktor, ed. *Die Korrespondenz Maximilians II.* Veröffentlichungen der Kommission für neuere Geschichte Oesterreichs 14, 16. Vienna: Holzhausen 1916–21.
Bothmer, Karl Freiherr von, and Georg Schnath, eds. *Aus den Erinnerungen des Hans Kaspar von Bothmer. Quellen und Darstellungen zur Geschichte Niedersachsens* 44. Hildesheim: Lax, 1936.
Droysen, Johann Gustav, ed. "Das Testament des grossen Kurfürsten."

Abhandlungen der philologisch-historischen Klasse der königlichen sächsischen Gesellschaft der Wissenschaften 5. 1870.

Dudik, B., ed. "Correspondenz Kaisers Ferdinand II. und seiner erlauchten Familie mit P. Martinus Becanus und P. Wilhelm Lamormaini." *Archiv für österreichische Geschichte,* no. 54, pt. 2 (1876): 221–350.

Ernst von Hessen-Rheinfels-Rotenburg. "Das Schicksal der Kinder Philipps des Grossmüthigen aus seiner Ehe mit Margaretha von der Saal." *Historisch-politische Blätter für das katholische Deutschland* 20 (1847): 93–95.

Heinrich Julius von Braunschweig-Wolfenbüttel. "Von der Susanna, wie dieselbe fälschlich von zweyen Alten des Ehebruchs beklaget, aber entlich durch Schickung Gottes . . . errettet, und die beiden alten zum Tode verdammet worden." *Bibliothek des litterarischen Vereins in Stuttgart* 36. Tübingen: Litterarischer Verein, 1855. 1–170 (first version); 171–208 (second version).

———. "Von einem ungeratenen Sohn welcher unmenschliche und unerhörte Mordthaten begangen." *Bibliothek des litterarischen Vereins in Stuttgart* 36. Tübingen: Litterarischer Verein, 1855. 335–400.

Kluckhohn, August, ed. *Briefe Friedrich des Frommen Kurfürsten von der Pfalz.* 2 vols. in 3. Braunschweig: Schwetschke, 1868–72.

———. "Das Testament Friedrichs des Frommen Churfürsten von der Pfalz." *Abhandlungen der historischen Classe der königlich bayerischen Akademie der Wissenschaften* 12, pt. 3 (1874): 41–104.

Köcher, Adolf, ed. Sophia of the Palatinate. *Mémoires. Memoiren der Herzogin Sophie nachmals Kurfürstin von Hannover.* Publikationen aus den königlichen preussischen Staatsarchiven 4. Leipzig: Hirzel, 1879.

Krause, Gottlieb, ed. *Urkunden, Aktenstücke und Briefe zur Geschichte der anhaltischen Lande und ihrer Fürsten unter dem Druck des 30 Jährigen Krieges.* 5 vols. Leipzig: Dyk, 1861–66.

Leibniz, Gottfried Wilhelm von. *Allgemeiner politischer und historischer Briefwechsel.* 7 vols. in 8. Darmstadt: Reichl/Akademie, 1923–1970.

Lenz, Max, ed. *Briefwechsel Landgraf Philipp's des Grossmüthigen von Hessen mit Bucer.* Publicationen aus den königlichen preussischen Staatsarchiven, 5. Leipzig: Hirzel, 1880–91.

Ludolf, Georg Melchior. *De introductione juris primogeniturae.* 3d ed. Jena: Bielck, 1733.

Lünig, Johann Christian, ed. *Das teutsche Reichs-Archiv.* 24 vols. Leipzig: Lanck, 1710–22.

Luther, Martin. *Die gantze Heilige Schrifft Deudsch.* 2 vols. 1545. Darmstadt: Wissenschaftliche Buchgesellschaft, 1972.

———. *D. Martin Luthers Werke.* 62 vols. Weimar: Böhlaus, 1883–1986.

———. *D. Martin Luthers Werke. Briefwechsel.* 18 vols. Weimar: Böhlaus, 1930–85.

Přibram, Alfred, and Moriz Landwehr von Pragenau, eds. *Privatbriefe Kaiser*

Leopold I an den Grafen F. E. Pötting 1662–1673. Fontes Rerum Austriacarum. Diplomataria et Acta 56, 57. Vienna: Gerold, 1903–04.

Saalfeldisches Recess-Buch: Die Verfassung des herzoglichen Sachsen-Gothäischen Gesammthauses die in demselben vorgenommenen Erbtheilungen, vornehmlich aber die . . . Sachsen-Coburg-Saalfeldischen Gerechtsamen betreffend. Coburg: Uhl, 1783.

Sachs, Hans. "Comedia. Jacob mit seinem bruder Esaw." Edited by Adelbert von Keller. *Bibliothek des litterarischen Vereins in Stuttgart* 102. Tübingen: Litterarischer Verein, 1870. 88–110.

Schulze, Hermann, ed. *Die Hausgesetze der regierenden deutschen Fürstenhäuser.* 3 vols. Jena: Fischer, 1862–83.

Stieve, Felix, ed. *Briefe und Akten zur Geschichte des dreissigjährigen Krieges.* vols. 4 and 5 of Abhandlungen der historischen Kommission der königlichen bayerischen Akademie der Wissenschaften. Munich: Rieger, 1878–95.

Urkundliche Quellen zur hessischen Reformationsgeschichte. 4 vols. Veröffentlichungen der historischen Kommission für Hessen und Waldeck 11. Marburg: Elwert, 1915–55.

Wendland, Anna, ed. *Prinzenbriefe zum hannoverschen Primogeniturstreit 1685–1701.* Quellen und Darstellungen zur Geschichte Niedersachsens 46. Hildesheim: Lax, 1937.

Books, Monographs

Altmann, Ruth. *Landgraf Wilhelm V. von Hessen-Kassel im Kampf gegen Kaiser und Katholizismus 1633–1637.* Marburg: Elwert, 1938.

Aretin, Karl Otmar Freiherr von. *Heiliges Römisches Reich 1776–1806: Reichsverfassung und Staatssouveränität.* 2 vols. Wiesbaden: Steiner, 1967.

Aries, Philippe. *Centuries of Childhood: A Social History of Family Life.* Trans. Robert Baldrick. New York: Vintage, 1962.

Aulinger, Rosemarie. *Das Bild des Reichstages im 16. Jahrhundert: Beiträge zu einer typologischen Analyse schriftlicher und bildlichen Quellen.* Schriftenreihe der historischen Kommission bei der bayerischen Akademie der Wissenschaften, no. 18. Göttingen: Vandenhoek und Ruprecht, 1980.

Beckmann, Johann Christoph. *Historia des Fürstentums Anhalt.* 3 vols. Zerbst: Zimmerman, 1710.

Below, Georg von. *Die Ursachen der Rezeption des römischen Rechts in Deutschland.* Munich: Oldenbourg, 1905.

Benecke, Gerhard. *Society and Politics in Germany 1500–1750.* London: Routledge and Kegan Paul, 1974.

Berger, Arnold E., ed. *Grundzüge evangelischer Lebensformung nach ausgewählten Schriften Martin Luthers.* Leipzig: Reclam, 1930.

Bezucha, Robert, ed. *Modern European Social History*. Lexington, Mass.: D. C. Heath, 1972.

Bireley, Robert, S. J. *Maximilian von Bayern, Adam Contzen, S.J., und die Gegenreformation in Deutschland 1624–1635*. Schriftenreihe der historischen Kommission bei der bayerischen Akademie der Wissenschaften 13. Göttingen: Vandenhoek und Ruprecht, 1975.

———. *Religion and Politics in the Age of the Counterreformation: Emperor Ferdinand II, William Lamormaini, S.J., and the Formation of Imperial Policy*. Chapel Hill, N. C.: University of North Carolina Press, 1981.

Blickle, Peter. *Landschaften im alten Reich*. Munich: Beck, 1973.

Bornhak, Conrad. *Deutsche Verfassungsgeschichte vom westfälischen Frieden an*. Stuttgart: Enke, 1934.

Bosl, Karl. *Bayerische Geschichte*. Munich: List, 1971.

———. *Die Geschichte der Repräsentation in Bayern*. Munich: Beck, 1974.

Carsten, Francis L. *Princes and Parliaments in Germany from the Fifteenth to the Eighteenth Century*. Oxford: Clarendon Press, 1959.

Cecil, Evelyn. *Primogeniture*. London: Murray, 1895.

Chaunu, Pierre. *La Civilisation de l'Europe classique*. Paris: Arthaud, 1966.

Dickmann, Fritz. *Der westfälische Frieden*. Münster: Aschendorff, 1959.

Dietrich, Richard, ed. *Politische Testamente der Hohenzollern*. Munich: Deutscher Taschenbuch Verlag, 1981.

Dollinger, Heinz. *Studien zur Finanzreform Maximilians I. von Bayern in den Jahren 1598–1618*. Schriftenreihe der historischen Kommission bei der bayerischen Akademie der Wissenschaften 8. Göttingen: Vandenhoek und Ruprecht, 1968.

Domke, Waldemar. *Die Viril-Stimmen im Reichsfürstenrath von 1495–1654*. Untersuchungen zur deutschen Staats und Rechtsgeschichte, no. 11. Breslau: Koebner, 1882.

Dreitzel, Horst. *Protestantischer Aristotelismus und absoluter Staat: Die "Politica" des Henning Arnisaeus (ca. 1575–1636)*. Wiesbaden: Steiner, 1970.

Dupâquier, J., E. Hélin, P. Laslett, and M. Livi-Bacci. *Marriage and Remarriage in Populations of the Past*. London: Academic Press, 1981.

Elert, Werner. *Morphologie des Luthertums*. 2 vols. Munich: Beck, 1931–32.

Esebeck, Frieda Freiin von. *Die Begründung der hannoverschen Kurwürde*. Quellen und Darstellungen zur Geschichte Niedersachsens, no. 43. Hildesheim: Lax, 1935.

Evans, R. J. W. *The Making of the Habsburg Monarchy, 1550–1700*. Oxford: Clarendon Press, 1979.

Feine, Hans. *Die Besetzung der Reichsbistümer vom westfälischen Frieden bis zur Säkularisation 1648–1803*. Kirchenrechtliche Abhandlungen, nos. 97–98. Stuttgart: Enke, 1921.

Ficker, Julius. *Vom Reichsfuerstenstände: Forschungen zur Geschichte der Reichsverfassung zunächst im XII. und XIII. Jahrhunderte.* 2 vols. Innsbruck: Wagner, 1861–1932.

Flandrin, Jean-Louis. *Families in Former Times: Kinship, Household, and Sexuality.* Cambridge: Cambridge University Press, 1979.

Franzl, Johann. *Ferdinand II: Kaiser im Zwiespalt der Zeit.* Graz: Styria, 1978.

Gebhart, Bruno. *Handbuch der deutschen Geschichte.* 9th ed. 4 vols. Edited by Herbert Grundmann and Karl Erdmann. Stuttgart: Union Verlag/Ernst Klett Verlag, 1970–76.

Gelbke, Johann Heinrich. *Herzog Ernst der Erste genannt der Fromme zu Gotha als Mensch und Regent.* 3 vols. in 1. Gotha: Perthes, 1810.

Giesey, Ralph. *The Juristic Basis of Dynastic Right to the French Throne.* Transactions of the American Philosophical Society, n.s., 51, pt. 5. Philadelphia: American Philosophical Society, 1961.

Glaser, Hubert, ed. *Um Glauben und Reich: Kurfürst Maximilian I.* Vol. 2 in 2 pts. of Wittelsbach und Bayern. Beiträge zur bayerischen Geschichte und Kunst. 3 vols. in 6 pts. Munich: Hirmer, 1980.

Glass, David, and D. E. C. Eversley, eds. *Population in History.* London: Arnold, 1965.

Goody, Jack, Joan Thirsk, and E. P. Thompson, eds. *Family and Inheritance: Rural Society in Western Europe, 1200–1800.* New York: Cambridge University Press, 1976.

Häberlin, Franz Dominicus. *Neueste teutsche Reichsgeschichte vom Anfange des Schmalkaldischen Krieges bis auf unsere Zeiten.* 20 vols. Halle: Gebauer, 1774–86.

Hartung, Fritz. *Volk und Staat.* Leipzig: Koehler and Amelang, 1940.

Hatton, Ragnhild. *George I: Elector and King.* Cambridge: Harvard University Press, 1978.

Heinemann, Otto von. *Geschichte von Braunschweig und Hannover.* 2 vols. Gotha: Perthes, 1884–86.

Hélin, Etienne. *La Démographie de Liège aux XVIIe et XVIIIe siècles.* Académie royale de Belgique. Classe des lettres. Mémoires 56, no. 4. Brussels: Palais des Académies, 1963.

Herrmann, Kurt. *Die Erbteilungen im Hause Schwarzburg.* Halle: John, 1919.

Herrschaft und Staat im Mittelalter. Wege der Forschung 2. Darmstadt: Gentner, 1956.

Holborn, Hajo. *A History of Modern Germany.* 3 vols. New York: Knopf, 1959–69.

Holl, Karl. *Die Bedeutung der grossen Kriege für das religiöse und kirchliche Leben innerhalb des deutschen Protestantismus.* Tübingen: Mohr, 1917.

Isenburg, Wilhelm Karl Prinz zu. *Europäische Stammtafeln: Stammtafeln zur*

Geschichte der europäischen Staaten, n.s. Edited by Detlev Schwennicke. 10 vols. Marburg: Stargardt, 1980.

Iserloh, Erwin, and Gerhard Müller, eds. *Luther und die politische Welt*. Historische Forschungen no. 9. Wiesbaden: Steiner, 1984.

Joliffe, J. E. A. *The Constitutional History of Medieval England*. 3d ed. London: Black, 1954.

Junge, Walter. *Leibniz und der sachsen-lauenburgische Erbfolgestreit*. Quellen und Darstellungen zur Geschichte Niedersachsens 65. Hildesheim: Lax, 1965.

Kawerau, Waldemar. *Die Reformation und die Ehe: Ein Beitrag zur Kulturgeschichte des 16. Jahrhunderts*. Schriften des Vereins für Reformationsgeschichte 39. Halle: Verein für Reformationsgeschichte, 1892.

Kisch, Guido. *Melanchthons Rechts- und Soziallehre*. Berlin: de Gruyter, 1967.

Klank, Wilhelm. *Die Entwicklung des Grundsatzes der Unteilbarkeit und Primogenitur im Kurfürstentum Brandenburg*. Borna: Noske, 1908.

Kleinman, Ruth. *Anne of Austria: Queen of France*. Columbus, Ohio: Ohio State University Press, 1985.

Koeppler, J. *Die Wirklichkeit der Domainien in Baiern*. Munich: Churfürstliche akademische Buchdruckerey, 1768.

Kraemer, Horst. *Der deutsche Kleinstaat des 17. Jahrhunderts im Spiegel von Seckendorffs "Teutschen Furstenstaat."* 1922–1924. Reprint. Darmstadt: Wissenschaftliche Buchgesellschaft, 1974.

[Krenner, Franz von] *Der Landtag im Herzogthum Baiern vom Jahre 1514*. N.p.: 1804.

Kruedener, Jürgen Freiherr von. *Die Rolle des Hofes im Absolutismus*. Forschungen zur Sozial- und Wirtschaftsgeschichte 19. Stuttgart: Fischer, 1973.

Kunst, Hermann. *Evangelischer Glaube und politische Verantwortung: Martin Luther als politischer Berater*. Stuttgart: Evangelisches Verlagswerk, 1976.

Lehmann, Hartmut. *Das Zeitalter des Absolutismus: Gottesgnadentum und Kriegsnot*. Stuttgart: Kohlhammer, 1980.

Lazareth, William. *Luther on the Christian Home*. Philadelphia: Muhlenberg, 1960.

Lewis, Andrew W. *Royal Succession in Capetian France: Studies on Familial Order and the State*. Cambridge: Harvard University Press, 1981.

Lojewski, Günther von. *Bayerns Weg nach Köln: Geschichte der bayerischen Bistumspolitik in der 2. Hälfte des 16. Jahrhunderts*. Bonner historische Forschungen 21. Bonn: Röhrscheid, 1962.

Lorimer, Frank. *Culture and Human Fertility*. Paris: UNESCO, 1954.

Mally, Anton Karl. *Der österreichische Kreis in der Executionsordnung des römisch-deutschen Reiches*. Wiener Dissertationen aus dem Gebiete der Geschichte 8. Vienna: Geyer, 1967.

McKeown, Thomas. *The Modern Rise of Population*. London: Arnold, 1976.

Mentz, Georg. *Weimarische Staats- und Regentengeschichte vom westfälischen Frieden bis zum Regierungsantritt Carl Augusts*. Part 1 of *Carl August. Darstellungen und Briefe zur Geschichte des Weimarischen Fürstenhauses und Landes*. Jena: Bidermann, 1936.

Moser, Johann Jacob. *Teutsches Staatsrecht*. 50 vols. Leipzig und Ebersdorff im Vogtland: Vollrath, 1737–53.

Naert, Emilienne. *La Pensée politique de Leibniz*. N.p.: Presses Universitaires, 1964.

Neveux, Jean Baptiste. *Vie spirituelle et vie sociale entre Rhin et Baltique au 17e siècle*. Paris: Klincksieck, 1967.

Noonan, John T. *Contraception: A History of Its Treatment by the Catholic Theologians and Canonists*. Cambridge, Mass.: Belknap, 1965.

Oestreich, Gerhard. *Neostoicism and the Early Modern State*. Edited by Brigitta Oestreich and H. G. Koenigsberger. Translated by David McLintock. Cambridge: Cambridge University Press, 1982.

Ozment, Steven. *When Fathers Ruled: Family Life in Reformation Europe*. Cambridge: Harvard University Press, 1983.

Parker, Geoffrey. *The Thirty Years' War*. London: Routledge and Kegan Paul, 1984.

Parker, Geoffrey, and Lesley M. Smith, eds. *The General Crisis of the Seventeenth Century*. London: Routledge and Kegan Paul, 1978.

Pass, Walter, *Musik und Musiker am Hof Maximilians II*. Wiener Veröffentlichungen zur Musikwissenschaft 20. Tutzing: Schneider, 1980.

Pfleiderer, Edmund. *Gottfried Wilhelm Leibniz als Patriot, Staatsmann und Bildungsträger*. Leipzig: Fue's Verlag, 1870.

Press, Volker, *Calvinismus und Territorialstaat: Regierung und Zentralbehörden der Kurpfalz 1559–1619*. Kieler historische Studien, no. 7. Stuttgart: Klett, 1970.

Rabb, Theodore K. *The Struggle for Stability in Early Modern Europe*. New York: Oxford University Press, 1975.

Raeff, Marc. *The Well-Ordered Police State: Social and Institutional Change through Law in the Germanies and Russia 1600–1800*. New Haven: Yale University Press, 1983.

Räss, Andreas. *Die Convertiten seit der Reformation*. 14 vols. Freiburg im Breisgau: Herder, 1866–80.

Riezler, Sigmund. *Geschichte Baierns*. 8 vols. Gotha: Perthes, 1878–1914.

Rockwell, William Walker, *Die Doppelehe des Landgrafen Philipp von Hessen*. Marburg: Elwert, 1904.

Rommel, Christian von. *Geschichte von Hessen*. 10 vols. Kassel: Perthes, 1820–58.

Rotberg, Robert I. and Theodore K. Rabb, eds. *Marriage and Fertility: Studies in Interdisciplinary History*. Princeton: Princeton University Press, 1980.

Rowen, Herbert. *The King's State: Proprietary Dynasticism in Early Modern France.* New Brunswick, N. J.: Rutgers University Press, 1980.

Schaer, Otto. *Der Staatshaushalt des Kurfürstentums Hannover unter dem Kurfürsten Ernst August 1680–1698.* Forschungen zur Geschichte Niedersachsens 4. Hannover: Geibel, 1912.

Schilfert, Gerhard. *Deutschland von 1648 bis 1789.* Berlin: Deutscher Verlag der Wissenschaften, 1962.

Schilling, Heinz. *Konfessionskonflikt und Staatsbildung: Eine Fallstudie über das Verhältnis von religiösem und sozialem Wandel in der Frühneuzeit am Beispiel der Grafschaft Lippe.* Quellen und Forschungen zur Reformationsgeschichte 48. Gütersloh: Mohn, 1980.

Schnath, Georg. *Geschichte Hannovers im Zeitalter der neunten Kur und der englischen Sukzession.* 2 vols. Hildesheim: Lax, 1938–76.

Schreiber, Otto. *Das Testament des Fürsten Wolfgang von Anhalt vom 25. August 1565.* Deutschrechtliche Beiträge, no. 9, pt. 2. Heidelberg: Carl Winter, 1913.

Schrötter, Ferdinand. *Abhandlungen aus dem österreichischen Staatsrecht und aus Freiheitsbriefen.* 5 vols. in 3. Vienna: Krauss, 1762–66.

Schulte, Aloys. *Der Adel und die deutsche Kirche im Mittelalter.* Kirchenrechtliche Abhandlungen 63 and 64. Stuttgart: Enke, 1910.

Schulze, Hermann. *Das Erb- und Familienrecht der deutschen Dynastien des Mittelalters.* Halle: Verlag der Buchhandlung des Waisenhauses, 1871.

———. *Das Recht der Erstgeburt in den deutschen Fürstenhäusern und seine Bedeutung für die deutsche Staatsentwicklung.* Leipzig: Avenarius and Mendelsohn, 1851.

Seckendorff, Veit Ludwig von. *Teutscher Fürstenstaat.* 5th ed. Frankfurt am Main: Götzen, 1708.

Shirer, William L. *The Rise and Fall of the Third Reich.* New York: Simon and Schuster, 1960.

Sieber, Eduard. *Die Idee des Kleinstaates bei den Denkern des 18. Jahrhunderts in Frankreich und Deutschland.* Basel: Basler Bücherstube Kobers Buch und Kunsthandling, A. G., 1920.

Skinner, Quentin. *The Foundations of Modern Political Thought.* 2 vols. Cambridge: Cambridge University Press, 1978.

Sohm, Walter. *Territorium und Reformation in der hessischen Geschichte 1526–1555.* Veröffentlichungen der historischen Kommission für Hessen und Waldeck 11, pt. 1. Marburg: Elwert, 1915.

Solé, Jacques. *L'Amour en occident à l'époque moderne.* Paris: Michel, 1976.

Spindler, Max, ed. *Handbuch der bayerischen Geschichte.* 2d ed. 4 vols. Munich: Beck, 1977–81.

Stollberg-Rilinger, Barbara. *Der Staat als Maschine: Zur politischen Metaphorik des absoluten Fürstenstaats.* Historische Forschungen, no. 30. Berlin: Duncker und Humblot, 1986.

Stolz, Otto. *Geschichte des Landes Tirol*. 1 vol. to date. Innsbruck: Tyrolia, 1955.

Strauss, Gerald. *Law, Resistance and the State: The Opposition to Roman Law in Reformation Germany*. Princeton: Princeton University Press, 1986.

————. *Luther's House of Learning: Indoctrination of the Young in the German Reformation*. Baltimore: Johns Hopkins University Press, 1978.

Tracy, James D., ed. *Luther and the Modern State in Germany*. Sixteenth Century Essays and Studies 7. Kirksville, Mo.: Sixteenth Century Journal Publishers, 1986.

Vehse, Edward. *Geschichte der deutschen Höfe seit der Reformation*. 48 vols. Hamburg: Hoffmann und Campe, 1851–60.

Viollet, Paul. *Histoire des institutions politiques et administratives de la France*. 3 vols. Paris: Larose et Forcel, 1900–03.

Vocelka, Karl. *Habsburgische Hochzeiten 1550–1600: Kulturgeschichtliche Studien zum manieristischen Representationsfest*. Veröffentlichungen der Kommission für neuere Geschichte Oesterreichs 65. Vienna, Cologne, and Graz: Böhlaus, 1976.

Walker, Mack. *Johann Jakob Moser and the Holy Roman Empire of the German Nation*. Chapel Hill, N. C.: University of North Carolina Press, 1981.

Werminghoff, Albert. *Der Rechtsgedanke von der Unteilbarkeit des Staates in der deutschen und brandenburg-preussischen Geschichte*. Hallische Universitätsreden 1. Halle: Niemeyer, 1915.

Zimmermann, Ludwig. *Der ökonomische Staat Landgraf Wilhelms IV*. 2 vols. Veröffentlichungen der historischen Kommission für Hessen und Waldeck 17, pts. 1 and 2. Marburg: Elwert, 1933–34.

Articles

Brady, Thomas, Jr. "The Political Masks of Martin Luther." *History Today* 33 (November 1983): 27–30.

Breitkopf, Johann Gottlob Immanuel. "Ueber Buchdruckerey und Buchhandlung in Leipzig." *Journal für Fabrik, Manufaktur, Handlung, und Mode* 4 (July 1793): 1–23.

Demandt, Karl E. "Amt und Familie." *Hessisches Jahrbuch für Landesgeschichte* 2 (1952): 79–133.

Dersch, Wilhelm. "Beiträge zur Geschichte des Kardinals Friedrich von Hessen." *Zeitschrift des Vereins für Geschichte und Altertum Schlesiens* 62 (1928): 272–330.

Dollinger, Heinz. "Kurfürst Maximilian I. von Bayern und Justus Lipsius." *Archiv für Kulturgeschichte* 46 (1964): 227–308.

Dülfer, Kurt. "Fürst und Verwaltung: Grundzüge der hessischen Verwaltungsgeschichte im 16.–19. Jahrhundert." *Hessisches Jahrbuch für Landesgeschichte* 3 (1953): 150–223.

Fichtner, Paula Sutter. "Dynastic Marriage in Sixteenth-Century Habsburg Diplomacy and Statecraft: An Interdisciplinary Approach." *American Historical Review* 21 (1976): 243–65.

Flandrin, Jean-Louis. "Contraception, mariage, et relations amoureuses dans l'occident chrétien" *Annales ESC* (1969): 1370–90.

Haake, Paul. "Ein politisches Testament König Augusts des Starken." *Historische Zeitschrift* 87 (1901): 1–21.

Houdaille, J. "Fécondité des familles souveraines du XVIe au XVIIIe siècle: Influence de l'âge du père sur la fécondité." *Population* 31 (1976): 961–70.

Koebner, Richard. "Die Eheauffassung des ausgehenden Mittelalters." *Archiv für Kulturgeschichte* 9 (1911–12): 136–98, 279–318.

Lüdtke, Wilhelm. "Veit Ludwig Seckendorf als deutscher Staatsmann und Volkserzieher des 17. Jahrhunderts." *Jahrbuch der Akademie zu Erfurt*, n.s., 54 (1939): 39–137.

Meinecke, Friedrich. "Luther über christliches Gemeinwesen und christlichen Staat." *Historische Zeitschrift* 121 (1920): 1–22.

Meisner, Heinrich Otto. "Staats- und Regierungsformen in Deutschland im 16. Jahrhundert." *Archiv für öffentliches Recht* 77 (1952): 225–65.

Muffat, Karl August. "Die Ansprüche des Herzogs Ernst, Administrators des Hochstiftes Passau, auf einen dritten Teil und an die Mitregierung des Herzogthumes Bayern." *Bayerische Akademie der Wissenschaften: Abhandlungen der philosophisch-historischen Klasse* 38 (1867): 113–44.

Näf, Werner. "Frühformen des 'modernen Staates' im Spätmittelalter." *Historische Zeitschrift* 171 (1951): 225–43.

Nischan, Bodo. "Calvinism, the Thirty Years' War, and the Beginning of Absolutism in Brandenburg. The Political Thought of John Bergius." *Central European History* 15 (1982): 203–23.

o Byrn, Friedrich August Freiherr. "Christian, Herzog zu Sachsen-Weissenfels, kursächsischer General-Feld-Marschall-Lieutenant." *Archiv für die sächsische Geschichte*, n.s., 6 (1880): 57–91.

Peller, Sigismund. "Studies on Mortality since the Renaissance." *Bulletin of the History of Medecine* 13 (1943): 427–61; 21 (1947): 51–101.

Pischel, Felix. "Die Entwicklung der Zentralverwaltung in Sachsen-Weimar bis 1743." *Zeitschrift des Vereins für thüringische Geschichte und Altertumskunde*, n.s., 20 (1911): 237–305; 21 (1912): 125–170.

Renner, Victor von. "Die Erbteilung Kaiser Ferdinand II. mit seinen Brüdern." *Zeitschrift des Ferdinandeums für Tirol und Vorarlberg*, 3d ser., 18 (1873): 197–248.

Ribbeck, n.n. "Landgraf Wilhelm IV. von Hessen auf der Brautsuche." *Zeitschrift des Vereins für hessische Geschichte und Landeskunde*, n.s. 23 (1898): 181–203.

Roper, Lyndal. "Luther: Sex, Marriage, and Motherhood." *History Today* 33 (December 1983): 33–38.

Schulze, Winfried. "Gerhard Oestreich's Begriff 'Sozialdisziplinierung' in der frühen Neuzeit." *Zeitschrift für historische Forschung* 14 (1987): 265–302.

Stone, Lawrence. "The New Eighteenth Century." *The New York Review of Books* 31, no. 5 (March 1984): 42–48.

Strauss, Felix. "Herzog Ernst von Bayern (1500–1560), ein süddeutscher fürstlicher Unternehmer des 16. Jahrhunderts." *Mitteilungen der Gesellschaft für Salzburger Landeskunde* 101 (1961): 269–84.

Sturmberger, Hans. "Die Anfänge des Bruderzwistes in Habsburg. Das Problem einer österreichischen Länderteilung nach dem Tod Maximilians II. und die Residenz des Erzherzogs Matthias in Linz." *Mitteilungen des oberösterreichischen Landesarchivs* 5 (1957): 143–88.

INDEX